*Difference Makers*

# Difference Makers
## AN *ACTION GUIDE* FOR JESUS FOLLOWERS

## M. SCOTT BOREN

**BakerBooks**

*a division of Baker Publishing Group*
Grand Rapids, Michigan

Published by Baker Books
a division of Baker Publishing Group
P.O. Box 6287, Grand Rapids, MI 49516-6287
www.bakerbooks.com

Printed in the United States of America

Library of Congress Cataloging-in-Publication Data
Boren, M. Scott.
    Difference makers : an action guide for Jesus followers / M. Scott Boren.
        pages cm
    Includes bibliographical references.
    ISBN 978-0-8010-1508-3 (pbk.)
    1. Evangelistic work. 2. Church work. I. Title.
BV3790.B6165 2013
261'.1—dc23                                                      2013004630

To the people and leaders
of Woodland Hills Church in Saint Paul, Minnesota.

Thank you for the opportunity
to be a part of a difference-making society.

# Contents

Contents

# Foreword

The moment anyone mentions kingdom work we gravitate toward the heroic and the magnificent. We may perhaps think of Augustine's colossal efforts, or the Reformers' powerful revolution, or the revivals under Jonathan Edwards, or Billy Graham's crusades, or the stories of the many authors whose books rocket onto the bestseller lists.

But Scott Boren's *Difference Makers* gently reminds us that kingdom work, the business of being difference makers and people of significant impact, does not begin on Wall Street or in Hollywood or Silicon Valley. It does not just happen back then or over there.

It begins at home, with your family; it begins in your neighborhood, with those around you; it begins in your church, with those with whom you worship weekly; and it begins at work, with those with whom you often spend your days. Difference makers, in fact, have concrete, ordinary strategies to reach out with God's love and grace to those around them.

A student of mine, deciding daily to remind himself of Jesus's summons to love God and love others in the ordinary ways of life, decided to befriend some homeless folks he had met. He decided to invite them to a party at his home. That one act of service and love led to a life of service and love—now he is in DC in a Christian ministry, making a difference and influencing many, including leaders of our nation. An ordinary act of compassion or service or love can unleash the grace of God and create a momentum of influence and difference.

What Scott Boren does in this book is this: he gives you forty days of short readings and exercises that, if done faithfully and adventurously and with openness to God's promptings, will lead you to the influence a follower of Jesus is meant to have. In fact, these readings could lead to substantive changes in your life and career. They certainly could lead you to do things you never dreamed of doing but are so glad you did.

In short, *Difference Makers* has the potential to lead you into the grand company of people who have been summoned by God to enter into the gospel work God is doing now—beginning with you and your neighborhood.

Scot McKnight

# Acknowledgments

Where do you begin when it comes to thanking people who contribute to the writing of a book? A book is much more than a set of ideas. It's an overflow of an author's heart, and authors are shaped by so many. Even though one name is on the cover, all books are really coauthored.

First, to Shawna, my partner in life and ministry, you are my muse, my inspiration. To our four children, my prayer is that I can pass on to you a life that I talk about in this book.

I owe so much to people who have shaped the specific words you read on these pages, especially my editors, Chad Allen, Rebecca Cooper, and Kristin Kornoelje. Thank you for all that you contributed. To those who offered critical feedback, Michael Mack, Gene Wilkes, Randall Neighbour, and A. J. Swoboda, I am grateful for your counsel and your help to get me unstuck in my words.

To the Father, Son, and Holy Spirit. This is your dance, after all. Thank you for including me in your love that makes all the difference.

# An Invitation

*The Father, Son, and Holy Spirit*

request the honor

of your presence

to participate in a journey

of becoming a difference maker

in your neighborhood

and within your networks

# Introduction

I can see our mailbox from the window of my home office. When the mail truck passes, an uncontrollable sense of anticipation rises within me. Might the carrier have a box for me? An unexpected package? An interesting catalog? With electronic communication and social media, I no longer expect personal communication in the form of letters or cards. However, one form of personal communication remains that arrives in a traditional envelope and printed on formal paper: an invitation.

You are holding a formal invitation of sorts. This book is inviting you to join the God who acts in this world to redeem all of creation. You are invited to embark on a journey to become a difference maker, something you will learn to be as you go.

While in my twenties, I lived in Vancouver, British Columbia. Within minutes of my apartment, I could be at the start of a number of hiking trails that led up a mountain, to a waterfall, or along a river. Having lived in various cities in Texas that did not have things such as expansive woods or mountainous trails, I was unaccustomed to taking journeys like this. I had to take on a new mind-set, one that fit in with hiking through forests and up mountains. I had to leave behind the expectations created by my experience of living on the rolling grasslands of Texas. I had to venture out, letting the tree-filled journey teach me along the way.

As you take this journey of becoming a difference maker, you can take action in one of two ways. Let's call the first a leap-of-faith action. Such action reflects those people who attack a trail or run up a mountain. Those who respond to God's invitation to make a difference in this way take action that is radical, substantial, or even wild. They don't just step out on the journey; they run it. If you are a radical who likes doing bold and passionate things for God, then go for it. However, most of us are not leapers.

The second kind of action is for the rest of us, for Jesus followers of the more ordinary sort. Let's call it a step-of-faith action. This kind of action requires us to put one foot in front of the other.

This is a step-of-faith action guide. Leap-of-faith radicals can implement these actions quickly and see results, but if we assume that it takes leaps of faith to make a difference, then most people—elementary school teachers, accountants, farmers, firefighters—will be left in the wings watching radicals who have the gumption, time, and freedom to take the leap. I'm inviting you to join me on a step-of-faith journey, one that frees all of us to follow Jesus into our neighborhoods and our networks and to live in a way that makes a difference.

## The Journey of E³ Difference Makers

When I moved to Vancouver, I could have just stayed in and watched television every Saturday. I had to choose to get up, turn off the television, and head out to a trail. The choices I made shaped my actions. On my first hike, I was tentative, but after two or three ventures on different trails, I began to look forward to my weekly outings. Hiking became a part of my life. In other words, my actions shaped my practices. And the more I hiked, the more hiking became a habit. The more I practiced hiking, the more it became a part of who I am. I became a novice hiker. When we repeat life practices, they become habits, and those habits become a part of our character.

The process works like this:

Choices
↓
Actions
↓
Practices
↓
Habits
↓
Character

As you read this book, use it as a trail guide. You will be challenged to make choices and then act on those choices. The more you act in those ways, the more your life will be shaped by those practices. And the more those life practices become a part of your regular rhythm, the more your character will demonstrate the life of a difference maker.

This action guide will point you to make choices that make a difference in three areas: encountering God, experiencing God together, and engaging the world with God. The story of Jesus washing the feet of the disciples from John 13 will help us see how these choices work. We encounter God as we allow Jesus to wash our feet. We experience God together as we wash one another's feet. We engage the world as we wash the feet of our neighbors.

We become difference makers as we are shaped by encountering, experiencing, and engaging. In other words, we are not trying to make a difference simply by implementing a set of tactics or strategies for changing the world. The way we encounter God makes a difference. The way we experience the love of being in a community makes a difference. The way we engage our world makes a difference. As we take steps in the three areas simultaneously, we grow as difference makers.

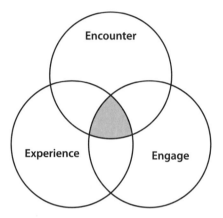

Instead of seeing these three parts as independent actions we take, we should see them as overlapping. When they overlap in our lives, difference making becomes a natural part of who we are.

encounter + experience + engage = $E^3$ difference makers

## Actions for the Journey

Some unique attributes of this book will help you make the appropriate choices. First, the book contains forty short readings designed to be read over a forty-day period. Since they are short, you can read them slowly. The readings are grouped into six parts. If you prefer to read larger chunks, then read each part in one sitting. As you read, it may be helpful to engage a three-step process:

1. Mark anything in the chapter that stands out to you.
2. Reflect on what you marked and ask the Lord to speak to you as you reflect.
3. Write down your thoughts on what stood out to you.

Second, each of the six parts contains an activity to do either by yourself or with a friend or two. Try to do as many as you can. The best way to learn is to act on what you are reading.

Third, if you are interested in going through this book with a small group of others, you can use the small group guide found in the appendix.

Finally, the opening page of each of the six parts contains a Scripture passage that is either a part of the story of Jesus washing the feet of the disciples or a part of the teaching that followed that act. This is provided to guide you in praying the Bible and listening to what the Spirit might be saying to you through the passage over a period of time. In this case, I'm inviting you to read the same passage each day for one week. Traditionally, this is known as *lectio divina*, an ancient way to listen to, to contemplate, and to pray the Scriptures so that the words of the Bible get deep within us and move us beyond the level of consuming information. Some call it "dwelling in the Word."

*Lectio divina*, or dwelling in the Word, can be challenging because most of us don't read Scripture this way. We might read a passage once and then pray about what we feel, but this process challenges us to read a passage four times, with a time of silence after each reading.

With the first reading, read the passage and listen to what it says, paying attention to anything that catches your imagination. After the second reading, you reflect on what stands out to you in the passage. This is followed by a third reading, after which you are invited to pray about whatever comes to your mind or heart in response to the passage. Finally, after the fourth reading, you are invited into a time of simply waiting with God in his presence.

When you first do this, it may feel weird to read the same passage four times followed each time by a period of silence. That feeling of weirdness is normal. Don't give up. The process may lead you to some new ways of connecting with God on this journey.

If you are reading this book with a group, have the facilitator read an introductory paragraph each time (samples are provided below) and then the passage. If you are doing this privately, you can follow the same pattern for the first few times until you get the hang of it.

Over the last few years, many experienced guides have written books on *lectio divina*. David Benner's *Opening to God* is one of the best. I have used his introductory words for each step, as they provide an excellent guide:

1. Read—Listen to what is written.

"Prepare now to hear God's Word to you. In this first reading, listen for the general sense of what is being communicated. Open your entire self to this process. Attend to the words you hear, but listen particularly for the word or phrase that stands out to you. Also notice any images that might form within you, or memories, sensations, or experiences that might arise in your consciousness as you listen. Sit in stillness after hearing the words and allow the Word of God to form within you as you open yourself in attentiveness and expectancy to what God has for you."[1]

Silence

2. Reflect—Take time to meditate on what stood out to you.

"Listen now to the same passage read a second time. This time allow yourself to ponder what you are hearing in both your head and your heart. Notice the thoughts that arise in response to the Word, and notice the movements in your heart."[2]

Silence

3. Respond—Offer your thoughts, emotions, and sensations back to God.

"Listen now to the passage a third time. This time allow yourself to respond to what has touched your mind and heart. This response may be worded or unworded, but it is prayer if it is offered with faith and openness to God."[3]

Silence

4. Remain—Wait before God in his presence.

"Listen to a final reading and allow yourself to simply be with God in stillness. Rest in God and be with the God who has spoken to you through the Word."[4]

Silence

Reading and praying the Scriptures in this way will prepare you for a life that makes a difference. It prepares your soul as you connect to God in deeper ways, and it also prepares you to love others in difference-making ways. While teaching a spiritual formation class on *lectio divina*, I saw a surprising connection between engaging Scripture in this way and engaging the world to make a difference. I realized that when I had been at my best in making a difference, I had been inadvertently applying these same four steps to how I served others. The best way to impact others is to love them through reading, reflecting, responding, and remaining. When I had fallen short of loving others, I had failed to engage others through these four steps that guide us on the journey and push us into a world that needs God's touch of redemption. The way we pray and the way we love are integrally connected. Let us pray and live to make a difference.

# Encountering
# *the* Difference Maker

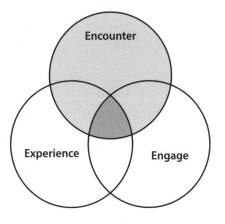

## *Lectio Divina* for Part 1

*Jesus knew that the Father had put all things under his power, and that he had come from God and was returning to God; so he got up from the meal, took off his outer clothing, and wrapped a towel around his waist. After that, he poured water into a basin and began to wash his disciples' feet, drying them with the towel that was wrapped around him. (John 13:3–5)*

**Read**

**Reflect**

**Respond**

**Remain**

# 1

## Putting Love Where Love Is Not

Something within us longs to see the world put right. Our hearts break when senseless violence results in a six-year-old girl being killed in a movie theater. Our frustration mounts when predators do harm to little boys. Our ire rises up when battered wives can't get out from under the thumbs of their husbands. We know that something is wrong with the world. We long for someone to stand up for what's right and good and beautiful.

Our fascination with superhero movies displays this longing. Since the release of *Superman* in the 1980s, the superhero genre has been one of the most popular. For instance, *The Avengers*—the third highest-grossing movie of all time—tells the story of a team of superheroes fighting to make things right. It's hard not to celebrate with them when their nemesis falls. In real life, we cheer on heroes who attack evil and stand out above the crowd to make a difference.

Imagine yourself at the end of your life. As you see yourself, think about where you live, the people in your life, and what you are doing. Reflect on the life you lived and the difference you made. Ask God to enliven your imagination. Think about how your life impacted others. How were others changed because of your influence? Do you wish you could have done more? Where did your actions fall short of what you wanted? What kind of a difference maker were you? (Write your reflections in the space provided at the end of this chapter.)

Every time I reflect on my life in this way, I think about George Bailey from the movie *It's a Wonderful Life*. George grows up in the small town of Bedford Falls and becomes somewhat of a local hero. He had dreams of doing great things, traveling the world, and getting a significant job in a significant city, but he got stuck taking care of the family business, the Bailey Building and Loan. After realizing that a large sum of money has been misplaced and that he could lose the Building and Loan, George's frustration grows to the point that he wishes he had never been born. In the rest of the movie, an angel named Clarence shows him what life would have been like if that had been the case. George gets to see what the town would have been like without him. In situation after situation, we see how people were positively affected by the simple actions of George Bailey, even though he saw himself as having little significance because he did not accomplish his big dreams.

Most difference makers have more in common with George Bailey than the heroes of *The Avengers*. They are ordinary people who make real differences in the small stuff of life, through the unseen actions that don't appear significant and most often go unnoticed. They connect with neighbors and meet little needs. They befriend a homeless person and allow him to shower in their home from time to time. They tutor a child who needs extra help.

However, the superhero trap invades our thinking. We assume that we have to do something big and noticeable to fix the world in order to make a difference. The call of the hero is the call to stand alone, to stand above the crowd, and to depend on one's own resources to change what's wrong. I always assumed that the real difference makers came in the form of preachers, foreign missionaries, and those who moved into the inner city to work with the impoverished. While I see no problem with taking on public roles that result in high-profile influence, we need to break the hero mentality and look at all the ways God works in our world.

St. John of the Cross wrote, "Mission is putting love where love is not." Even though I have secretly desired to be a Christian avenger, a caped hero who does good when everyone else can't, Jesus invites us to this simple yet difficult call. When Jesus came to earth, he did not come as a caped hero with superpowers that allowed him to force his goodness on others. We are told that he emptied himself of the powers and privileges of the Creator (Phil. 2:6–8). He came as one of us and offered love in places that lacked love. He came as a servant and revealed the nature of God through the scandal of the cross (1 Cor. 1:23). The tool God used to redeem creation and turn around the mess of the world was love.

We cannot change our messed-up world—including marriages that are falling apart and kids who cannot learn because their parents are never home, or public issues such as human trafficking and racially driven violence—if we try to *force* others to line up with what is right. God invites us to embody his way of *being* love so that we might engage our neighborhoods and networks with that love.

The apostle Paul said something like that when he wrote:

> If I speak in the tongues of men or of angels, but do not have love, I am only a resounding gong or a clanging cymbal. If I have the gift of prophecy and can fathom all mysteries and all knowledge, and if I have a faith that can move mountains, but do not have love, I am nothing. If I give all I possess to the poor and give over my body to hardship that I may boast, but do not have love, I gain nothing. (1 Cor. 13:1–4)

As you imagine yourself a few decades from now reflecting on the difference you made with your life, what do you see? What imprint did you make on the world? Take a few minutes and ask God to make you into the kind of person who puts love where love is not. This is the stuff that changes the world.

Write down your thoughts from the imagination exercise.

# 2

## Participating in God's Difference

Francis has been in the church for most of her ninety years. Recently, she realized that most of the people in her life outside the church were not Christians and had little interest in going to church. In a Bible study discussion, she reflected on how much time Jesus spent in homes talking with people over meals. So she started inviting some of her friends and neighbors to her home for tea. After a few times, she invited a younger church friend to join her. She openly shared her experiences with God, her life in the church, and how she encounters God in prayer. A few weeks later, a couple of her neighbors volunteered to help in the church kitchen and even visited a church worship service. Francis participated in something quite different from her previous ways of doing church.[1]

The Bible begins with "In the beginning God . . ." The climax of the Bible is all about what God did when Jesus came to earth to reveal the character of God's love and then died and rose again. The end of the Bible is about how God will restore all of creation and reveal the new heaven and earth. God is the primary actor. He initiates. He is the main character of the story, and he is the producer of the story. He is the One who holds together the various actors who never seem to quite get what God is doing through them in his story.

I am not the protagonist of God's story. In fact, I am not even a main character. This does not diminish my importance or value. It is simply an acknowledgment of the fact that God acts and initiates, and our action is simply a response to his initiation.

While it's easy to write these words, I find it much more challenging to live by them. When it comes to the question of how we can make a difference in the world, we focus on trying to find tactics and strategies. We look for programs that can deal with poverty. We put our trust in mentoring strategies to get kids off the streets. We develop systematic evangelism tactics and train people to go out and evangelize. We are concerned with trying to find answers to questions such as:

What can I do to serve the poor?

How can I better fulfill my calling?

How can I share the gospel message?

How can I advance God's kingdom this week?

Then we ask the ultimate question: What would Jesus do to minister to others if he were physically here on earth today?

At first glance, these questions seem right. After all, the Bible commands us to focus on things such as justice, ministry, and servanthood. Jesus is our model. Why not ask, What would Jesus do? However, underneath these questions lies a subtle snare. These noble questions trap us in a rule-following approach to making a difference. Instead of allowing God to initiate difference making, we champion a list of rules about what serious Christians should be doing to make a difference.

I've been around people like this. On the surface, their work is admirable. They move into the inner city and work with those who live in under-resourced neighborhoods. Or they invest their lives in orphans, widows, and the homeless just as the Bible says to do. However, when you listen to them, it seems as though no one can live up to their standard. They judge themselves and everyone else who does not do what they do.

In contrast, I have friends who invest their lives in the same ways, but their approach is 180 degrees different. They do it because they are following Jesus into the neighborhood. They have no time to judge those who don't do what they do because their focus is on Jesus. They resemble Francis, the ninety-year-old church lady who saw a way to join God in loving the people around her. They are participating with God in his work of turning the world around, and they are allowing God to reshape their lives so that they are more fully difference makers.

In contrast to following a set of rules or tactics, difference makers follow Jesus by encountering God's love, experiencing love as they work together, and engaging others with this love. This is E³ difference making.

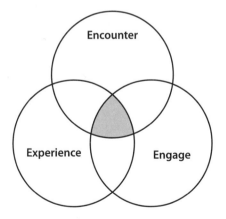

31

Difference makers act out of the middle. Francis encountered God working in Scripture in a way she had not seen before. She engaged her neighbors and experienced life together with both unbelievers and another Christ follower. She experienced $E^3$ difference making, the place where difference making naturally and organically flows.

# 3

## Dancing with God

When I was a freshman in high school, I went to a student convention in Houston. Somehow we convinced our teacher to take us dancing at Gilleys. Yes, that's right, Gilleys is the seedy honky-tonk bar that is the setting for *Urban Cowboy*, starring John Travolta and Debra Winger. Because I grew up in a conservative Christian church, country and western dancing was not at the top of my to-do list. In addition, I have two left feet. But I wanted to learn to dance. Luckily, three very patient girls were kind enough to teach me.

I will never forget that first time on the dance floor. One of the girls picked a slower song so I could pick up the beat, and then she showed me the basic two-step. I learned very quickly that being a good follower meant I could not look down at my feet. When I looked down, I inevitably stepped on my partner's feet. To learn to dance, I had to look at my dance partner and learn to be sensitive to subtle shifts.

God's difference makers are dancers because God dances. The Father, Son, and Spirit share life in an interconnected way that resembles an eternal relational dance. The perfect loving union of the Father, Son, and Spirit is an eternal unity of the being we call God. Difference makers dance the dance with God.[1]

The apostle Paul concluded his second letter to the Corinthian church by writing, "May the grace of the Lord Jesus Christ, and the love of God, and the fellowship of the Holy Spirit be with you all" (13:14). The dance of the Trinity opens up to us and invites us to participate in what God is doing.

Another dance I learned that night is called the three-step. It's not as popular as the two-step, but it's great for beginners. Since difference making requires us to join God in fresh, unexpected ways, even those who have been Christians for years have to begin at the beginning with these three basic dance steps:

Step 1: God in me. This step focuses on the question, How is God transforming me?

Step 2: God ahead of me. With this step we ask, What is God already doing in the world?

Step 3: God through me. Here we ask, What does God want to do?[2]

The first step is about our personal encounter with God, something we commonly emphasize. However, if we stop there, we might get our marching orders from God to be a difference maker, but then we are left to ourselves to figure out how to carry out those marching orders. We need all three steps to dance with God and thereby live out the character of difference makers. Jesus illustrated this quite clearly. In John 5, Jesus tells his followers, "My Father is always at his work to this very day, and I too am working" (v. 17). God the Father is at work in the world to redeem his creation. The dance of the Father, Son, and Spirit weaves redemptive love throughout the world. God is dancing on your street and in the lives of your neighbors. God is dancing in the schools near you, at the places where you work, and with your family members.

In that same conversation, Jesus stated, "Very truly I tell you, the Son can do nothing by himself; he can do only what he sees his Father doing, because whatever the Father does the Son also does" (v. 19). This is a remarkable statement. If Jesus, God incarnate, operated in this fashion, how much more should we? The Son of God lived in friendship with the Father by the power of the Spirit, and this shaped how he lived, ministered, and related to other human beings. This mind-set shaped how Jesus operated, and it shapes how God moves through his people today.

Tracy had one semester left in Bible school. She had plans, and her friends assumed that God had great things for her. Then her mother, who did not know God, became ill and needed significant surgery. As Tracy was dancing with God, she discovered a new compassion for her mom and decided to move back home to take care of her. None of her friends at school understood her decision, but that's where the dance of God's unpredictable love led Tracy.

One early church teacher, Irenaeus of Lyons, called the Son and the Spirit the hands of God extended to do the work of the Father on earth. When we enter into the mystery of God's love, the Father extends his arms to us and draws us in. Then we can see how the Spirit goes ahead of us and is already at work in the world, and we can see how the Son and the Spirit work their power in us to extend God's love to a loveless world.

God extends his hands to us, invites us onto the dance floor of our neighborhoods, and begins to teach us the dance of putting the world right side up again. How does that happen practically? Well, that's the purpose of the rest of this book.

## Part 1 Activity

**Dancing in Your Neighborhood**

Set aside fifteen to thirty minutes to take a walk around the area in which you live. Before you go, ask the Lord to give you his heart for the people who live there. As you walk, ask the three-step questions:

1. How is God transforming your attitude toward your neighborhood?
2. What is God already doing?
3. What does God want to do?

Ask the Holy Spirit to enliven your heart and mind to see more of what God sees. When you get back home, record your thoughts.

# 4

## Inside Out Difference Makers

While working as a youth intern during college, I attended an evangelism training event at Baylor University. Before the kids arrived for the event, all the youth pastors and leaders took part in some intensive evangelistic training sessions. One night I walked to a local convenience store to purchase a snack, and I met a homeless man. I bought him some food and told him about Jesus. He even prayed the prayer to accept Jesus. Who knows? He could have done it to get me to leave. After all, I was on the Christian conference passion drug and was probably rather pushy.

This experience increased my passion even more. It was as if I had crossed over some kind of Rubicon. Even though I had led others to Jesus before, I was jumping through the ceiling. I felt like a real Christian.

Looking back on that experience, I now realize how I turned the act of sharing Jesus into something I did for myself, not for the man I met that night. I was doing a good thing for the wrong reasons. Look at me. Look what I did. I was doing all the stuff I had been trained to do, but being a person who reflected God's character of love was not on my radar screen.

In the book *Friendship at the Margins*, Christopher Heuertz tells of his experience of sharing life with the marginalized poor of society. He writes, "If we want people to experience the kingdom of God and to dwell with God for eternity, then how they experience their relationship with us should be a foretaste of that goodness and beauty."[1] People need more than a message about God and salvation. They need to see and taste the love of God through us. Heuertz and his coauthor, Christine Pohl, continue, "Mission, then, is less about our efforts to help or evangelize 'them,' and more about how we can live into the kingdom together. Friendship puts the focus on relationships and offers an alternative to models of mission that are more formal, professional, and bureaucratic."[2]

We can join God in sharing friendship with others because God has befriended us. We love because he first loved us. We are on a mission to make a difference in the world because we have been transformed from the inside out. Because being a difference maker is about *who we are* and not just *what we do*, we need ongoing, fresh encounters with the God of love to make difference making possible. This may seem obvious, but it seems to me we often miss this fact and assume that we outgrow the need for the transforming touch of God. The story of Jesus washing the feet of his disciples points us in the right direction:

> It was just before the Passover Festival. Jesus knew that the hour had come for him to leave this world and go to the Father. Having loved his own who were in the world, he loved them to the end.
>
> The evening meal was in progress, and the devil had already prompted Judas, the son of Simon Iscariot, to betray Jesus. Jesus knew that the Father had put all things under his power, and that he had come from God and was returning to God; so he got up from the meal, took off his outer clothing, and

wrapped a towel around his waist. After that, he poured water into a basin and began to wash his disciples' feet, drying them with the towel that was wrapped around him.

He came to Simon Peter, who said to him, "Lord, are you going to wash my feet?"

Jesus replied, "You do not realize now what I am doing, but later you will understand."

"No," said Peter, "you shall never wash my feet."

Jesus answered, "Unless I wash you, you have no part with me."

"Then, Lord," Simon Peter replied, "not just my feet but my hands and my head as well!"

Jesus answered, "Those who have had a bath need only to wash their feet; their whole body is clean. And you are clean, though not every one of you." For he knew who was going to betray him, and that was why he said not every one was clean. (John 13:1–11)

Jesus was the unveiling of God, the coming of God's fullness in a way that had not happened before. Jesus shocked the disciples (and us) by pulling back the curtain on God's character by showing us that God is a foot-washing God. The way Jesus made a difference in the world was by taking on the lowest of all roles and serving. This flies in the face of all logical expectations of what a god should look like. John tells us that all power had been given to Jesus, and the way he displayed this power was by washing feet. This does not fit any definition of power I know about.

Read the story from John 13 again. As you do, think about which person in the story you identify with most readily. I connect with Peter. In my gut, I don't want a God who takes off his outer garment, puts on a towel, and washes my feet. I want a God who can do something about the situation. I want a God who can set things right. Honestly, I want God to be like the Avengers and put his power on display so that I can have a piece of that power for myself to make things better. As long as God manifests his power with control and authority, those who line up with him get to be mini-avengers. However, the actions of Jesus subvert this mind-set, and he destabilizes the way we think authority should work.[3]

Peter couldn't see how God could manifest power in weakness. He needed a transforming encounter with Jesus to change him from the inside out. Today, we also need to allow God to wash our feet, to serve us with his transforming love. It's the way we are transformed so that we can be difference makers.

# 5

# What Kind of God?

Words are tricky. Different people can read the same words and understand them in vastly different ways. For instance, what do you think of when you hear the word *caribou*? For most people, it's simply a large animal that resembles a moose. For me, it means coffee, because when we lived in Minnesota, we frequented coffee shops by that name. "Drinking Caribou" has special meaning to me that just sounds weird to most people.

Here are some tricky words: "For God so loved the world" (John 3:16). It's the most popular verse in the Bible, but what does it really mean? These words mean different things to different people based on their personal experiences. When you read John 3:16, what do you think of when you hear the word *God*? Don't think theologically. You can give all of the right theological responses, but if you go deeper and look in your heart, there you will find your feelings about God. What's the first thing that pops into your head? What feelings does God have toward you? What do you experience when you think about God?

Take a few minutes to do the following activity. For this activity to work, you have to be completely honest with yourself. Don't think in terms of what *should* be but what really is. When you think about God, do you envision God being more like the words above the line or below the line? Put a mark on the line that represents your experience of God. For most people, they mark somewhere in between the two extremes.

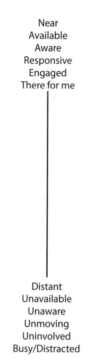

Near
Available
Aware
Responsive
Engaged
There for me

Distant
Unavailable
Unaware
Unmoving
Uninvolved
Busy/Distracted

Now do the same thing for these two sets of words. When you think about God, is God more like the words on the left or the words on the right? Put a mark somewhere along the line that represents your experience of God.

| Scary | Good |
|---|---|
| Angry | Kind |
| Threatening | Caring |
| Unsafe | Gentle |
| Judgmental | Forgiving |
| Punishing | Safe |

Now let's put these two graphs together. Plot the intersection of your two points. Your dot should be in one of the four quadrants. For instance, if your mark was lower on the first line and to the right on the second, then your dot will be in the lower right-hand quadrant.

Near
Available
Aware
Responsive
Engaged
There for me

Scary
Angry
Threatening
Unsafe
Judgmental
Punishing

Good
Kind
Caring
Safe
Forgiving
Gentle

Distant
Unavailable
Unaware
Unmoving
Uninvolved
Busy/Distracted

These four quadrants correspond with four general experiences or perceptions of God. They are:

Authoritative (upper left): This perception of God sees him as being highly involved in our lives but also very judgmental and authoritarian. This kind of God is invasive. He has a plan for our lives and we had better get it right.

Benevolent (upper right): This perception of God sees him as engaged in our lives and nonjudgmental. He is highly involved while at the same time caring and forgiving.

Critical (lower left): This perception of God sees him as judgmental and disengaged. He is distant and uninvolved while at the same time severe and demanding.

Distant (lower right): This perception of God sees him as nonjudgmental and disengaged. He is like the nice uncle figure who is uninvolved and has no opinion about our lives. He is too distant and distracted to have a direct impact on our lives.

According to the research done by Baylor University sociologists Paul Froese and Christopher Bader and reported in their book *America's Four Gods*, the American population is spread out almost equally under these four perspectives. For instance, my tendency is to see God as authoritative, even though I have worked for years to reenvision God and see him as revealed in Scripture. For many reasons, my brain naturally goes to a place that sees God as judgmental and controlling. I have realized that if I don't continually meet with God and allow him to retrain my brain on a regular basis about who he is, the kind of God I show others—from my kids to my neighbors—will also be judgmental and controlling.

Our love of others—whether neighbors, co-workers, friends, or family—will never extend beyond the love we experience from God. Left to yourself, you will engage your neighbor with the kind of love you imagine God offering you. If you see God as judgmental and harsh, you will judge others. If you see God as distant and uninvolved, then you will be likewise. If you perceive God as the great Santa Claus in the sky, then—well, you get the picture.

All Christians believe God makes a difference, but your picture of God will shape the kind of difference you think he should make. If you view God as the grand, all-powerful One who does whatever he wants to get people to do the right thing, then you might imagine difference makers as super-Christians who swoop in with great authority and have special gifts to get people to do the right thing. They may look more like the Avengers, who have good intentions, but their special abilities are not used in self-sacrificial ways. They overcome the power of evil with the same kind of power. Washing feet is not the preferred way of making a difference.

On the other hand, if you encounter the radical, sacrificial love of God—much like Peter did when Jesus washed his feet—you will know the God who serves. You will be much more likely to engage others with humility and sacrificial servanthood. You will have more power to enter into conversations and offer friendship, even with those you would not naturally befriend. As God washes your feet, you can join him in washing the feet of the world.

# 6

## What Is God Already Doing?

We encounter God vertically—God in us—which is the first step of our dance with God. The second step leads us to ask, What is God already doing? This is the dance step of God ahead of us.

As you drive through your neighborhood, where do you see God already at work? When you walk past co-workers, what do you see God doing? While sitting with your family at the dinner table, what do you see God already doing? How is God going ahead, weaving his love into unexpected places?

Sometimes we relegate God's work to things we consider "sacred" and leave God out of those things we label "secular." We look for God to work inner healing, personal salvation, and freedom from moral sin, all of which we desperately need. However, we don't see what God is already doing all around us because we don't expect God to show up in things such as family events, our relationships with our neighbors, our work, the local schools, city counsel meetings, or local businesses.

God's love goes forth in this world in unexpected places. Maybe you meet at a local restaurant with a Christian friend to have a "spiritual" conversation. What is God doing in that local restaurant? What's happening in the life of the waitress who serves you? How might God use that place to reveal his love? We could ask the same kinds of questions about our homes, our schools, our workplaces, or the bleachers at a Little League park.

God's arms of love extend everywhere. We don't have to think about how to invite people to a "spiritual" event or meeting so that they can find God's love. Of course, they should be welcomed to attend such meetings, but we need to embody a way of love that sees God ahead of us and allows for conversations to happen everywhere, even outside those meetings.

Part of the problem is the way we use the word *love*. Just as everyone's brain responds differently to the word *God* (see previous chapter), our brains also have various reactions to the word *love*. In cultures that use English as their primary language, the word *love* is used for all kinds of things. While we use the one word *love* to mean a wide array of emotions, actions, and vague notions, the Greek language has four words that allow for much more specific and nuanced usage.

The New Testament speaks of love in a very specific and unique way, especially when we consider the various ways these four words were used in the first-century culture. The first word, *storge*, is not used in the Bible, but it refers to the fondness or affection we might have for something because we have become familiar with it and it brings value to us. For instance, I "love" baseball. I "love" good Mexican food. I "love" to read a good book or watch a great movie. We are fond of these things because we are comfortable with them or approve of their characteristics.

*Philos* lies behind the word *Philadelphia*, "the city of brotherly love." It refers to friendship love or companionship. In this experience of love, people find that they are sharing a common journey with others, often a journey they did not expect. Companions are not made as much as they are discovered. While a few places in the New Testament use this word, it is not used to refer to God's unique kind of love for his people.

Many of us know the third word, *eros*. It is the basis for the word *erotic*. This love occurs when two people turn toward each other and focus attention on the other because they are "in love." In eros, feelings, passion, and physical intimacy are involved. In the true sense of the word, such physical intimacy is not about selfish fulfillment. Eros is about wanting the beloved, about desiring intimacy with the other, who is the focus of our attention. Of course, erotic love has been perverted to simply describe the act of physical intimacy for personal pleasure without any reference to intimacy with the beloved.

The last word used for love is *agape*. Before the New Testament was written, this word was used in a variety of ways, and as a result, it did not have a concrete, stable meaning. Scholars suggest that the New Testament writers chose this word so that they could give it concrete meaning and fill it out with the kind of love that God is. If, then, *agape* is an undefined word, how do we know what it means? What defines love? First John 3:16 states, "This is how we know what love [agape] is: Jesus Christ laid down his life for us." Agape love is Jesus hanging on a cross, dying for those who hated, rejected, and misunderstood him. Agape is other-oriented, self-sacrificial, and choice-based love.[1] It stands in stark contrast to the other three kinds of love. Storge represents fondness for someone or something. Eros speaks to romantic passion. Philos is about preferential companionship. But agape is defined by the giving of self completely, as Jesus did on the cross.[2]

Agape love meets people on their turf, in the same way that Jesus came and met people on the turf of the world. Jesus continues to meet people in unexpected places and unexpected ways. In every culture, there are places where beauty, truth, and agape love are already flowering. And in every culture, there are those who are expressing their longing for that beauty, truth, and love. They know that something is missing. Both are revelations of God's work ahead of us. How do we recognize this? The famous love chapter penned by the apostle Paul in 1 Corinthians describes the nature of agape love. I've taken Eugene Peterson's translation and modified it to describe God's agape character, replacing "love" with "God." Where we see these things happening, we see God. When we hear people longing for these things, they are calling out for God. Here is how it reads:

God never gives up.
God cares more for others than for himself.
God doesn't want what he doesn't have.
God doesn't strut,
God doesn't have a swelled head,
God doesn't force himself on others,
God isn't always "me first,"
God doesn't fly off the handle,
God doesn't keep score of the sins of others,
God doesn't revel when others grovel,
God takes pleasure in the flowering of truth,
God puts up with anything,
God believes in others,
God always looks for the best,
God never looks back,
God keeps going to the end. (based on vv. 4–7)

Take a few minutes and read this again slowly. Stop where you sense the Lord speaking to you. Write down your thoughts.

# 7

## What Does God Want to Do?

Randall has four friends who have little interest in God-talk. He has been praying for them for over twenty years. He does not preach to them, although he does not hide his relationship with Jesus. He loves them because he has experienced the God who loves him unconditionally. God's kindness led him to repentance, and because of that reality, he can offer the same kindness to his friends. He is a difference maker because he is putting love where love is not.

Will these people come to know Jesus? I hope so. However, the love Randall and his wife extend to them is not conditional. They love because they have been shaped by love. That's what love does. They embody a way of life in their neighborhood that is attractive and beautiful, not so that people will come to church—although they hope they will eventually worship God—but because this way of life fits what it means to be God's people. It's what God's people do. They don't do it because it works. They do it because it's the way love works.

This leads us to the third dance step: God through us. We participate in this part of God's dance as we ask the question What does God want to do?

To help us get our minds around this, let's learn some Latin. *Missio Dei* simply means "the mission of God" or "God's mission." Isaiah 61:1, 3 contains a great summary of the *missio Dei*:

> The Spirit of the Sovereign LORD is on me,
>> because the LORD has anointed me . . .
> to bestow on them a crown of beauty
>> instead of ashes,
> the oil of joy
>> instead of mourning,
> and a garment of praise
>> instead of a spirit of despair.
> They will be called oaks of righteousness,
>> a planting of the LORD,
>> for the display of his splendor.

When Jesus began his earthly ministry, he read this passage, and then he said, "Today this scripture is fulfilled in your hearing" (Luke 4:21). Jesus began a new work of God, displaying and announcing that God had come to set things right. Then, after he ascended, he sent the Spirit to continue this work in the world. This is the *missio Dei*.

The arms of God come to bring the beauty of love, restoration, hope, freedom, and wholeness into the "ashes" of despair, brokenness, isolation, and bondage. God's mission is to restore his creative beauty to a world that sin, hatred, and selfishness have taken over. Practically speaking, there is much that God wants to do all around you. Kids at local schools need mentors. Homeless people need support. Those caught in sex trafficking need advocates. Battered women need help. The unemployed need direction. Those entrapped in generational poverty need guidance. In all of these cases, these people need friends; they need to experience God through you and me. This is what God wants to do. Look around. See what's going on and invite God to do something marvelously shocking through you.

When the Spirit works through us, God's character shapes our character. We may start out doing things to make a difference because it's the right thing to do, but then we realize after some time has passed that we are different. The Spirit has reshaped who we are. We have shifted from doing good things for people who need help to loving those people sacrificially. We look in the mirror and realize that we are actually looking more and more like difference makers.

If we look again at the characteristics of agape love, we can apply them to what it means to be God's people, just as we applied them to what it means to understand God's character:

God's people never give up.

God's people care more for others than for themselves.

God's people don't want what they don't have.

God's people don't strut,

God's people don't have swelled heads,

God's people don't force themselves on others,

God's people aren't always "me first,"

God's people don't fly off the handle,

God's people don't keep score of the sins of others,

God's people don't revel when others grovel,

God's people take pleasure in the flowering of truth,

God's people put up with anything,

God's people believe in others,

God's people always look for the best,

God's people never look back,

God's people keep going to the end.

We recognize difference makers by this list. This is who God is shaping to set the world right.

# Experiencing a Difference-Making Team

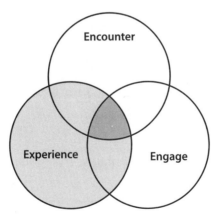

## *Lectio Divina* for Part 2

*A new command I give you: Love one another. As I have loved you, so you must love one another. By this everyone will know that you are my disciples, if you love one another. (John 13:34–35)*

**Read**

**Reflect**

**Respond**

**Remain**

# 8

# Me? A Difference Maker?

History books focus on people who made a difference in the world. People such as George Washington, Wolfgang Amadeus Mozart, Thomas Edison, and Albert Einstein left their fingerprints on the world. When I think about people who changed the world, names such as Nelson Mandela, Martin Luther King Jr., Mother Teresa, and Gandhi come to mind. As I reflect on previous centuries, names such as St. Francis of Assisi, John Wesley, and William Carey stand out.

The story of Jackie Pullinger also impresses me. In 1966, she felt led to be a missionary in Hong Kong, even though no mission agency would support her. She started out as a teacher in the part of Hong Kong that was then one of the largest opium-producing areas in the world. Over the years, she and others who are a part of the ministry she started, the Saint Stephen's Society, have helped thousands of drug addicts, prostitutes, and gang members change their lives.

I ask myself, Can I make that kind of difference in the world? I must be honest. I'm no Mother Teresa. I'm not that interested in being stuck in a jail unjustly like Nelson

Mandela. And the spiritual leadership of John Wesley blows me away. These difference makers inspire me, but I'm not sure I can measure up to their heroic standard.

Heroes start movements and mobilize masses of people. It's easy for us to look at them and hold them up as models for the rest of us to emulate. We try to be radical. We aim to be zealous for Jesus. We stir up passion. Then, after a while, we run out of energy. We just don't seem to have what it takes to really make a difference in the world.

Mother Teresa once said, "There are no great acts, only small things done with great love." As I read about the early church and how it grew under great oppression, I discovered this same perspective. The incredible growth of the early church in the Roman Empire changed history. The church grew from three or four hundred followers of Jesus after the resurrection to over thirty million people three centuries later. Talk about impact! How did this happen?

There are many reasons, but one has come to light in recent years through some very detailed historical analysis. History tells us that the Roman Empire was hit by widespread disease multiple times that wiped out thousands of citizens. Roman citizens who had the means fled the towns and cities hit with the disease. Those without financial means quarantined themselves from their family members who were infected and waited for them to die. But records tell us that Christians cared for those who were ill, even nonbelievers abandoned to die. Medical historians tell us that survival was higher for those given care and nourishment. Many of those left to suffer and die became believers because of Christians who cared for them while putting their own lives at risk. Simply because care was given, the church grew.[1]

We do not have the names of the people who served the sick and dying during the dark days that plagued the Roman world. We don't have a list of those who prayed for sick neighbors, brought them food, and sat with them at the risk of their own well-being. But these anonymous Jesus followers changed the world forever because of these simple acts. Can we not do the same today?

Imagine your pastor announcing a new strategy for your church: "Let's become a group of people who suffer and die for the sake of people who reject Jesus. God is calling us to wash the feet of the world, and more specifically the feet of our neighbors. This is not just something for the leaders and clergy to do. It is something for all of us because this is how we come to know God."

While this might not be a popular approach, it seems that this is the perspective of Jesus when he said, "Whoever wants to be my disciple must deny themselves and take up their cross daily and follow me. For whoever wants to save their life will lose it, but whoever loses their life for me will save it. What good is it for someone to gain the whole world, and yet lose or forfeit their very self?" (Luke 9:23–25). We all can participate in this, even in small ways, because this is the way of discipleship. And no one is excluded from that invitation.

Now you are not Mother Teresa and you never will be. The good news is that you don't have to be. You can join God in making a difference in a way that lines up with the way God made you. And most likely, it will come about in small, unnoticed ways that touch people's lives—mentoring a child at a local school, helping a single mom with her kids, having conversations with a neighbor who medicates himself with alcohol, inviting some people from work over to dinner. I'm not sure that the Christians who cared for those inflicted with disease that spread throughout the Roman Empire ever realized the kind of impact that their lives had. They were just doing "small things with great love." They just loved and served because that's how the love of God works through God's people. They lost their lives for the sake of the world, and the world changed. Today, it's no different.

# 9

## Your Unique Difference

When I travel and speak at a church, often people will say something like, "Oh, you're from Houston? I love Joel Osteen. I watch him on TV every week. It's remarkable the kind of impact he has." Now, of course, not everyone likes him. Maybe you prefer Chuck Swindoll, Joyce Meyer, or John Piper. Whatever our choice, we find it easy to identify with a big-name speaker or leader who is helpful. Don't get me wrong. I'm not against great preaching, nor do I believe we need to do away with church leadership. However, the modern celebrity status of speakers highlights a centuries-old pattern that pervades even the smallest of churches. It's called sacradotalism. Sacradotalism is when people look to an official leader to do the ministry for them in return for their attendance at meetings and an offering. Sacradotalism requires that these leaders have the complete package and can minister to any and everyone in any and every situation.

Jesus could have been a celebrity Christian leader. He could have ministered to people on his own. But instead, he sent out his disciples to engage people and proclaim the presence of

God's kingdom in the midst of life. And he never sent them out alone. One of the most vivid examples of this is found in Luke 10, where Jesus sent out seventy-two of his followers in pairs. It reads:

> After this the Lord appointed seventy-two others and sent them two by two ahead of him to every town and place where he was about to go. He told them, "The harvest is plentiful, but the workers are few. Ask the Lord of the harvest, therefore, to send out workers into his harvest field. Go! I am sending you out like lambs among wolves. Do not take a purse or bag or sandals; and do not greet anyone on the road.
>
> "When you enter a house, first say, 'Peace to this house.' If someone who promotes peace is there, your peace will rest on them; if not, it will return to you. Stay there, eating and drinking whatever they give you, for the worker deserves his wages. Do not move around from house to house.
>
> "When you enter a town and are welcomed, eat what is offered to you. Heal the sick who are there and tell them, 'The kingdom of God has come near to you.'" (vv. 1–9)

Jesus observed that "the workers are few." Even though God incarnate was walking around on earth healing, forgiving, and teaching, he did not do these works alone. He empowered others to work together to extend his ministry.[1]

When we hold back and look to those who hold official positions to do what needs to be done, the world is the lesser for it because each of us has something unique to contribute. No one can replace you. No one can do something the way you can.

This is one of the reasons why difference-making teams are so crucial. When you are alone, the pressure is on you. When you work with others, the load is lighter. You can do what you are good at while others do what they are good at.

Simon and I had not been friends for very long before he told me of his struggle with homosexuality. His previous experience with church had been filled with judgment, condemnation, and rejection. I wanted to offer a different experience. The best part about this story is that I did not have to have all the answers, because I had very few. Simon also shared his story with Quan, which meant that at least two of us could walk with Simon through the ups and downs of his journey.

Quan had a different way of investing in the friendship than I did. None of us is wired in the same way, and therefore we will all impact the world in different ways. This should be obvious, but when our view of church has been shaped by sacradotalism, sometimes we set ourselves up for failure. We establish unrealistic expectations about the kind of difference maker we are supposed to be. We assume that we have to be good at everything in order to minister to others.

Interestingly enough, this assumption pervades the way we think about all kinds of areas of life. The Gallup organization has performed research on this in many sectors of society. They have found that most people have a tendency to put their energy into strengthening the weaknesses in their lives. If they are great motivators but weak administrators, they assume they need to develop their administrative skills. Polls found that when an individual operates in his or her area of unique strength while letting other people do the other tasks, productivity increases dramatically.[2]

Of course, this insight is really not new. The apostle Paul said something very similar about two thousand years ago. In his first letter to the Corinthians, Paul said, "There are different kinds of gifts" (12:4). But this means that we have to learn how we are gifted and allow the Spirit of God to flow through us in those ways. We cannot look at the gifts that seem more important and envy them. Paul put it this way:

> The eye cannot say to the hand, "I don't need you!" And the head cannot say to the feet, "I don't need you!" On the contrary, those parts of the body that seem to be weaker are indispensable, and the parts that we think are less honorable

we treat with special honor. And the parts that are unpresent-
able are treated with special modesty, while our presentable
parts need no special treatment. But God has put the body
together, giving greater honor to the parts that lacked it, so
that there should be no division in the body, but that its parts
should have equal concern for each other. If one part suffers,
every part suffers with it; if one part is honored, every part
rejoices with it. (vv. 21–26)

You have something unique to offer the world, and that
uniqueness works best when joined with others on a mission.
You do not need to live up to an image of an ideal Christian.
You can be yourself and offer who you are, and God will use
the team to make his kind of difference.

Reflect on the things you enjoy and do well and make a
list of them. In what areas do you need the contributions of
others? List some of them.

# 10

## Called Together

"But you are a chosen people, a royal priesthood, a holy nation, God's special possession, that you may declare the praises of him who called you out of darkness into his wonderful light" (1 Pet. 2:9). The "you" in this sentence is plural. It is not talking about who you are as an individual. It is about who you are as a part of God's people. As a part of the family of God, we are a part of a new nationality, a new citizenship, a new way of living. We are chosen to be a part of this people, who are priests to the world together.

This is the way Jesus ministered with his companions, the twelve disciples. When he sent out his followers, he sent them out to minister in pairs. He never sent them out alone. The apostle Paul ministered with a group of people who included Barnabas, Silas, Timothy, and Luke.

God forms us together in order to be a group of difference makers. In some cases, it is two people. In others, it is a small group of ten or twelve. In others, it is a group of twenty-five or thirty.

Jesus understood the importance of working together and tried to get his disciples to see this after he washed their feet. Let's return to that story:

> When he had finished washing their feet, he put on his clothes and returned to his place. "Do you understand what I have done for you?" he asked them. "You call me 'Teacher' and 'Lord,' and rightly so, for that is what I am. Now that I, your Lord and Teacher, have washed your feet, you also should wash one another's feet. I have set you an example that you should do as I have done for you. Very truly I tell you, no servant is greater than his master, nor is a messenger greater than the one who sent him. Now that you know these things, you will be blessed if you do them. (John 13:12–17)

The way of self-sacrifice, the way of servanthood, the way of the cross that Jesus embodied is not merely a message that makes for great sermons. His point goes beyond our talk about God. It's how we are to be with one another. The act of washing feet reveals who God is, and it opens our eyes to see how we were designed to live. We were made to give love away. We were made to experience—giving and receiving— agape love with others.

Jesus not only tells the disciples to wash each other's feet but also adds this teaching: "A new command I give you: Love one another. As I have loved you, so you must love one another. By this everyone will know that you are my disciples, if you love one another" (John 13:34–35). In other words, the way the world will know that they are followers of Jesus is through the way they love one another.

Jenny was a small group leader who had a passion for sharing life together. She modeled this by being transparent about her own life. After a period of months of doing this, she grew weary because none of the others reciprocated. So she told her pastor she wanted to go back to leading the group as an informational Bible study. During the next meeting, there were two visitors, friends of group members, who did not know Jesus. As the meeting progressed, one group member opened up and shared that he had contracted the HIV virus through sexual experiences. His shame had caused him to hide his condition. At that point, walls came down all over the room. People cried. People shared. And then one of the visitors confessed that this was just too much for her, and she left. The other said, "I'm overwhelmed by this. But if this is what it means to follow Jesus, I want to join you."

In John 17, Jesus prayed for his closest disciples, and then he prayed for the people who would later become disciples and be a part of the church. This prayer was answered in Jenny's meeting that night: "My prayer is not for them [the disciples] alone. I pray also for those who will believe in me through their message [future disciples], that all of them may be one, Father, just as you are in me and I am in you. May they also be in us so that the world may believe that you have sent me" (vv. 20–21).

The way the world will come to know that Jesus was sent by the Father to reveal the heart of God is by our love for one another. Difference makers are a part of a difference-making society. If you want to serve people at a homeless shelter, then go with a friend or go as a small group. If you want to mentor a child at a local elementary school, find someone with a similar longing and go together. If you want to invest in a family in need, then work with a few other people. Don't think about what you can do. Think about what God wants to do through a group of his people.

This applies to everything we will be talking about in the rest of this book. Consider how God wants to minister through you to your neighbors. If you spend time with them by yourself, you might have some influence on them. If you collaborate with a friend or two, your prayers for your neighbors will increase, you will have more fun, and others will see the life of Jesus *among* you, not just *in* you. You will have more creative ideas about how to serve your neighbors, and you will have others who can stand with you as you do it.

## Part 2 Activity

### A Conversation with a Friend

Meet with a friend to talk about what God is doing and wants to do in the community around you. Here are some questions to guide your conversation:

- What has God been doing in you that motivates you to have this conversation?
- What unique gifts do you think you have to offer others in the neighborhood?
- What do you see God already doing in your neighborhood?
- What are some things you think God wants to do?

# 11

## Opening Our Hearts to Work Together

The way we Christians love one another is the way we will love our neighbors. However, when people look at the church at large, unified love does not first come to mind. All kinds of things have divided the church over the centuries, and often local congregations are not much better. Unity that reflects the love of the Trinity, the kind that Jesus prayed the church would experience (see John 17), is often more of a pipe dream than a reality. So we settle for something like "being nice to one another" instead of really experiencing God's agape love with one another.

After Jesus washed his disciples' feet, he told them that the mark of his followers would be their love for one another. You may think this is good for those who are called into full-time ministry like the disciples. Or it may have worked for these men because they were with Jesus for three years. However, let's remember who these men were. These were the rough and tumble of society: fishermen, a zealot (a mercenary who fought against the Romans), a Roman tax collector, and others like them. Jesus gathered a group of individuals who would not have been friends unless something larger called them into unity. These were not cultured individuals who gathered to do religious things together. Jesus's words that their agape love would be a sign to the world were wildly radical.

His words challenge us when we so easily get our feelings hurt in the church. They also challenge the notion that unity has to be experienced only with people we like. The reality is that we can live in unity with all kinds of people as long as we are committed to the same vision, the vision of making a difference with God.

At the same time, we live in a culture in which we tend to keep others at arm's length. God has put in all of us a yearning for unity, but most of us don't know how to actually experience it. Then we make excuses like, "We have to know people for a long time before we can walk in unity," or "I just don't trust people naturally." We need a way for people who are committed to living out God's kingdom of agape love and making a difference in our world to taste unity.

What if we tried something different? What if we took a risk that challenged us to open up our lives to one another?

Paul's instruction provided in his letter to the Colossians gives us some insight into the experiment I've seen bring unity to people who would not naturally connect:

> Therefore, as God's chosen people, holy and dearly loved, clothe yourselves with compassion, kindness, humility, gentleness and patience. Bear with each other and forgive one another if any of you has a grievance against someone. Forgive as the Lord forgave you. And over all these virtues put on love, which binds them all together in perfect unity. Let the peace of Christ rule in your hearts, since as members of one body you were called to peace. And be thankful. Let the message of Christ dwell among you richly as you teach and admonish one another with all wisdom through psalms, hymns, and songs from the Spirit, singing to God with gratitude in your hearts. (3:12–16)

Notice that this passage is written to a group of people. We cannot have compassion, kindness, humility, gentleness, and patience while isolated. Reread the last sentence. Paul challenges individuals to be full of Christ so that they can encourage one another. We can all do this, even when we don't feel like it or don't realize we have something to offer others, because the power of the Spirit lives within us.

Here's a way to experience the reality of this passage with a couple of friends or an official small group:

Step 1: Over the next few days, seek an encounter with God by yourself in a way that is meaningful to you. Break the normal pattern of praying. Go for a walk and talk to God as you experience nature. Listen to a CD while you drive and worship God. Read a devotional book and write a journal entry. Find a painting online of Jesus on the cross and look at it while you pray and thank God for your salvation. The key is to find something that works for you.

Step 2: This experience with God can serve as your contribution to the group. If you connected with God in a song, bring the CD and play it. If you read something in a book that really spoke to you, read it aloud and share why it had meaning for you. Maybe you went for a walk and picked up a rock along the way. Bring that rock and share what you experienced on your walk. If you wrote in your journal, share an entry. If you painted something, show it. If you were touched by a poem, read it. If you saw a movie that touched you, play a clip.

You need not be profound or deep. The point is to share your experience with God with others. This insight will feed the group prayers, and it will connect you with others. Our vulnerability will always speak to others. By simply sharing our connection with God, we build one another up and experience what Paul wrote about.

Here are some basic guidelines for this activity.

• When you meet, there is no Bible study per se. This is an invitation for people to share what they have to offer.

- Read Colossians 3:12–14. Someone should share that this is a time to practice this passage, not to study it.
- Open the floor for people to share voluntarily what they have brought to the group.
- The group must be committed to listening to what each person offers. For some, this is a very vulnerable experience. Affirmation is crucial.
- The focus of the sharing should come out of each individual's encounter with God. This is not a time of preaching or instructing. If someone goes down that track, he or she needs to be steered in a different direction.
- Whatever is shared should have an encouraging tone. This is about experiencing the love of God, not about religious performance or condemnation. If someone shares a condemning experience with the group, listen, but also help them to hear God's love for them.

# 12

## Making Time for Difference Making

Ray Kroc developed a brilliant business model in the 1950s with the development of the drive-thru window, but this mind-set goes far beyond our eating habits. The drive-thru window serves as a metaphor for how normal life works for a large segment of the population. We are always in a hurry. We want things now. We don't like to wait. Unfortunately, such attitudes inhibit our ability to hear the Spirit's leading in our day-to-day activities. We lack the time and space for making a difference.

Romans 12 says, "Do not conform to the pattern of this world, but be transformed by the renewing of your mind" (v. 2). The word *conformed* points to those things that happen to us from the outside. Like Jell-O in a mold, we fit into the shape the world gives us. Every time someone asks, "So how's it going?" we answer, "Wow! Life has been crazy." If we don't consider how we do life, the Jell-O mold of our culture will dictate how we live.

In contrast, the word *transformed* refers to what happens on the inside of us and what moves us to impact the world around us. Instead of the fast-food life controlling us, we make time in our lives to make a difference. Instead of going with the flow, we go against the flow. Difference makers carve out time to receive God's love through prayer, worship, and Bible reading so they can impact others with God's love. They value the experience of God's love with other Christians so they can make a difference together.

For many, a lack of time is one of the most challenging obstacles to making a difference. Jobs are demanding. Families are pulled in many directions. And the pressures to make ends meet keep us stressed. Going against the flow is not easy. If you try to add a difference-making activity to your already packed life, how much can you really do? Let's say you start mentoring a child at a local school. You may think it will take only an hour every week and you can squeeze that in, but this kid is a person, not a block of time. What are you going to remove from your life so that you have enough emotional space to be a difference maker in someone's life?

Asking this question can be intimidating at first. You may think that everything you do is important. However, when we take a look at one week in our lives, we can see that we can give up one television show or spend less time on Facebook. We can manage our time at work better and not put in as much overtime.

The challenge of time pressures is one of the main reasons why difference-making teams are so crucial. As we step out with God, we find ourselves not able to do as much as we want to do for people in need. We need partners who can pick up the slack when we can't, and we need people who can help us think through how we spend our time so that we can make a difference.

I'm not challenging you to revamp how you do your day-to-day life. I'm just inviting you to say no to one or two things that are currently in your schedule so that you have room to begin to make a difference in meaningful ways in the life of someone else. I'm inviting you to make a little room in your life to have a cup of coffee with a hurting friend, to go for a regular walk in your neighborhood, or to host a cookout for your neighbors.

To think this through, use the following chart to reflect on the last week and how you spent your time. You don't need to include the details, just list what you did during the morning, afternoon, and evening. Try to list the people you engaged with in those activities. Then pray and be open to what the Lord might show you.

## Weekly Schedule

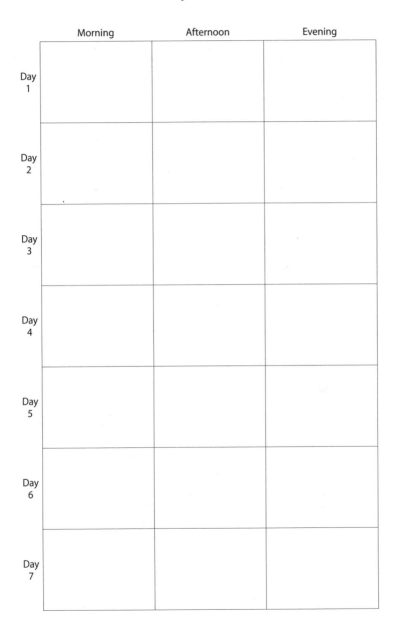

|  | Morning | Afternoon | Evening |
|---|---|---|---|
| Day 1 |  |  |  |
| Day 2 |  |  |  |
| Day 3 |  |  |  |
| Day 4 |  |  |  |
| Day 5 |  |  |  |
| Day 6 |  |  |  |
| Day 7 |  |  |  |

# 13

## Making Room for the Team

During my first couple of years of walking with Jesus, I met weekly with Bryan. He mentored me through some ups and downs in my walk with God. For a few months, his work took him to a different city. During that time, he returned for a weekend visit. That's when I heard a knock at the door. I almost fell to the floor when he walked into my apartment. I could not believe he had made time to hang out with me. I don't remember anything we talked about that day. Words did not matter. Bryan had room for me in his life, and that made all the difference in the world to me. As long as I've known him, he's lived in a way that provides room for him to make a difference in others' lives. This also makes it easier for him to work with teams in the calling to be a difference maker in the world.

As I have stated, being a difference maker is best done in a team of difference makers. However, if we have no time for becoming a team, then how can we actually work together as a team? Most teams form as they work together. Deep friendships are developed as we walk side-by-side. But we must do more than work together. The experience of God's love through one another takes time as we connect and share life. This cannot be done as we squeeze others into our already busy lives.

Many things squeeze out the room in our lives to make a difference. We discussed how we use our time in the previous chapter. Money pressure can also steal our ability to make a difference. While in my midtwenties, I decided I wanted to trade in my eight-year-old car for a new one. It did not take long to find one I liked. The payments were doable, and I was ready to make the deal, but I thought I would ask God what he had to say about the situation. That night, I sat under a starlit sky and had a conversation with God, mostly about how much I wanted a new car. In the stillness, I heard back, "I have other uses for that money." I said, "Really? Are you sure? But . . ."

I wish I could say I was thrilled because I had heard direction from God, but I did not get the answer I wanted. Little did I know that about a year later a door would open for me to further my Bible training at a school in Canada, and I would have an opportunity to serve in a significant volunteer role in a church there. If I had had a four-hundred-dollar car payment, that move would have been much more difficult, maybe even impossible. At the very least, I would have been strapped to multiple jobs just to pay the bills, and I would have missed out on the rich relationships with teams that developed as we served together.

Difference makers are resident aliens in their neighborhoods. We may be citizens of a country such as the United States, Canada, or England, but we are actually resident aliens because our citizenship is in the kingdom of God. As citizens of God's kingdom, we are challenged to form our lives around the ways of the kingdom. The Message translates 1 Peter 2:9–10 this way:

> But you are the ones chosen by God, chosen for the high calling of priestly work, chosen to be a holy people, God's

instruments to do his work and speak out for him, to tell others of the night-and-day difference he made for you—from nothing to something, from rejected to accepted.

When we choose to make God the center of our lives, we open our lives up to God's meddling. God wants to get involved in those areas that we tend to set aside as belonging to the realm of personal choice. God sees what we don't see, and his desires do not always make sense in the moment. When we don't understand how he's leading, we don't usually like what he says.

We cannot let our feelings in the moment dictate our decisions. Nor can we allow the expectations of everyone else to control us. We need to develop the diligence to hear God and follow hard after what he is saying.

Here's a practical way to do that. Look back at the exercise in chapter 12. Rank the things you wrote down according to their level of priority. You can even color code these four priority levels:

1. Absolutely essential
2. Important but not essential
3. Helpful but not necessary
4. An extra that is fun if I have time

Why do this? So you can increase God's love in your life. So you can connect with God. So you can make time for a friend. So you can have some down time and take a walk. So you can offer your time to someone who really needs it. So you can have some extra cash when a need of a neighbor comes to light. This is not only about giving up something so you can have a better life. It's also about giving up something so that others can experience something better from your life. This way we make room to work with others and create the space in our lives to enjoy one another as we work together.

# 14

## The Reality of Teamwork

I have a friend who jokes, "Ministry is great, except for the people." God's kind of ministry is all about the people. That's what makes it so great, and it's also what makes it so challenging. Our culture teaches us that we should all strive to be self-sufficient, autonomous individuals. When we try to work together, that individualism fights against the call to walk in unity. We are pulled to make decisions about life in isolation from others and to try to make it on our own without community. Working together to make a difference is a lot more fun, but it's also a lot of work.

I've yet to find any perfect people. Therefore, relationships never work as we wish they would. This means there is no ideal church. There are no ideal small group experiences. There are no ideal team experiences. People let us down. They hurt us, sometimes purposefully. We are caught in the reality that God is shaping his church to be a people of agape love even though, at the same time, sin is present.

We can observe this on multiple levels as we work together as difference makers. First, there are normal relational conflicts. As we work with others, we see things differently. We communicate differently. Personalities rub us the wrong way. We misunderstand one another. Sometimes we get angry with others. The question facing us is how we will respond to these episodes of conflict.

God is revealing himself through these experiences, not in spite of them. God is not waiting for the ideal church to arise or the perfect small group to develop so that we can then go forth and make a difference. This is the beauty and the power of God. The Bible refers to us as "saints" even though we fall short of this reality on a daily basis. As we struggle to grow up and allow the Spirit to move in us so that our reality reflects this sainthood, the love of God is revealed. God is not looking for nice churches. God is working through the messes we create along the way to reveal his love. Therefore, when we encounter differences, we work through them, find God together, and see what God is doing in the midst of them. The way we handle our conflicts may be the way we show our neighbors what God's love looks like.

On another level, a much more tragic and painful experience can block our ability to work together. In his book *Faith in Real Life*, Mike Tatlock writes, "Looking deep into the church, many see only hypocrisy, judgmentalism, anger, selfishness, greed, and pride. For many, the church has blood on its hands."[1] If the thought of working with others churns negative feelings within you, you are not alone. Sadly, hurting church people have hurt a lot of other people through the years. If you find yourself in this situation, part of your journey will include forgiving those who have hurt you. If you don't let go of your hurt, you will only perpetuate the problem.

If you find yourself in this place, let me offer a couple of suggestions. First, learn to forgive in a healthy way. Forgiveness does not mean you need to let those people continue to hurt you. When you forgive, you are simply letting go of them and what they did to you. Holding on to the pain will not help you. It will only cause you to hurt others.

78

Second, if unsafe patterns of people hurting others have taken over and poisoned you and those close to you in the church, try to find one safe person and begin to share life in Christ with him or her. Refuse to complain about the church. If that is not possible, seek God's leading about where you should worship. Ask the Lord to empower you to forgive those who have hurt you.

In extreme cases in which you experienced spiritual abuse, controlling leadership, or a church culture that was dominated by leaders who perpetually hurt people, seek wise counsel and direction.[2] You will need to experience a time of healing and discover a different form of church leadership that embodies the way of Christ washing feet.

Whatever the case, every group, team, and church goes through ups and downs. Even in the best of situations, you will hurt others and get hurt by others. That's just the way it works. How you respond in these situations is the important thing, because the way you respond is a way of demonstrating God to the world.

# Engaging Your World by Paying Attention

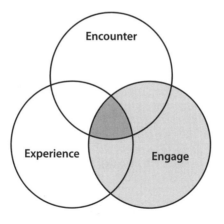

*When he had finished washing their feet, he put on his clothes and returned to his place. "Do you understand what I have done for you?" he asked them. "You call me 'Teacher' and 'Lord,' and rightly so, for that is what I am. Now that I, your Lord and Teacher, have washed your feet, you also should wash one another's feet. I have set you an example that you should do as I have done for you. Very truly I tell you, no servant is greater than his master, nor is a messenger greater than the one who sent him. Now that you know these things, you will be blessed if you do them."* (John 13:12–17)

**Read**

**Reflect**

**Respond**

**Remain**

# 15

## Restful Force

I'm an avid fan of baseball. Over the course of a long season, even the best players experience what's called a hitting slump. It refers to an extended period of not hitting the ball well. Unlike in basketball or football, where players break out of below-average performances with additional aggression or a time of rest so they can return with more aggression, the approach in baseball is different. Aggression actually works against you in baseball. Hitting a ball consistently is about allowing your mind and body to relax so that you can swing in a fluid motion. When hitters overswing, they miss the chance to apply the restful force that results in a hard-hit ball. Restful force. It's counterintuitive, but the best way to hit the ball is to focus on allowing your body to rest so that the right force can be applied.

The writer of Hebrews wrote about this oxymoronic concept by saying, "There remains, then, a Sabbath-rest for the people of God; for anyone who enters God's rest also rests from their works, just as God did from his. Let us, therefore, make every effort to enter that rest, so that no one will perish by following their example of disobedience" (4:9–11).

Honestly, I was puzzled by this passage for years. I'm one of those type A, goal-setting people who bite off way more than they can chew. Then, after all the work, all I want to do is veg in front of the TV. Work or rest. That's my tendency in life, and that's how I tried to understand this passage. Obedience to God is work. Ministry is work. Serving the poor is work. Reaching unbelievers is work. Conducting worship services is work. Preaching is work. Then, after I'm exhausted from making a difference, I rest.

I've realized that my type A aggressive tendencies rarely line up with what God is doing. His ways offer us a pattern of ministry of "making every effort to enter that rest." The Spirit of God works with restful force. Our greatest effort should be to enter that kind of rest daily. We fight to enter that rest so that we can participate in what God is doing to make a difference.

A few years ago, I realized that I was around far too many Christians like me who have the same aggressive approach. While we were trying to make a difference in the world, we were neglecting things such as our children, our marriages, and our neighbors, and we were not fun to be around. I realized that this way of life was not beautiful, winsome, or alluring. It was a way of life that actually turned people away from God instead of drawing them in.

Restful force allows us to flow with what God is doing. The means of the ministry line up with the end. The way we make a difference must line up with the results we want to see from our ministry. We want people to encounter Jesus and take on the way of life that aligns with Jesus. We want to offer people more than ourselves, more than our best efforts. Therefore, we need a way to engage people with this restful force of Jesus.

I discovered this pattern as I was learning the discipline of *lectio divina* explained in the introduction and that hopefully you have been practicing while reading this book. This way of reading the Bible helps us enter into the imagination of the Bible. It causes us to slow down and listen to what the Spirit may be saying to us through the Bible. Let's review the four steps of *lectio divina*:

1. Read—Listen to what is written.
2. Reflect—Take time to meditate on what stood out to you.
3. Respond—Offer your thoughts, emotions, and sensations back to God.
4. Remain—Wait before God in his presence.

After a time of reading the Bible in this way, I saw a correlation between how we effectively engage our neighborhoods and the love of God. When I have benefited from a powerful ministry, the person or persons ministering took this approach. Every time I have ministered to others in a way that had a lasting impact, I took this approach. I don't think any of us mapped this out as a strategy. Most likely, the circumstances and the relationships were such that this kind of ministry flowed naturally. The four steps of engaging our world look like this:

1. Paying attention—Listening and seeing the needs and what God is already doing in the world.
2. Reflecting—Praying in a way that we can be directed by God to take the kind of action he would have us take.
3. Acting—Responding to the needs we observe in visible, concrete ways.
4. Being a faithful presence—Remaining with the people and in the places as a society of difference makers.

Difference makers don't hurry or force their ways on others. Instead, they pay attention to the real needs being expressed. They listen to God to see how the Spirit may be leading them to respond. This is followed by a faithful response, not a prepackaged, canned response they learned from someone else. And finally, they continue the relationships they develop through the ministry.

My hope and prayer is that we can make it a regular practice to enter into God's rest as we participate with God in making a difference. As we walk together through the rest of this book, you will discover how these four steps equip you to be difference makers in your world.

How have you experienced this pattern of ministry?

# 16

## Paying Attention

Communication research has demonstrated that what people say constitutes only a part of what they are actually communicating. Some suggest that up to 93 percent of communication actually comes in the form of nonverbal cues. What goes unsaid says far more than we realize.

I have developed a bad habit of responding to the buzzers and sounds of my iPhone when in the company of others. I have refined my ability to do multiple things at once, including listening to others while seeing who emailed me. But the fact is that when I respond to my iPhone, I'm not paying full attention to the person in my presence. My daughter lets me know this when she inserts her head in the small space between my phone and my face.

Paying attention. This is crucial to reading our neighborhoods well. God is at work in our world. The Spirit moves, but reading what the Spirit is doing requires that we pay attention to the whispers and nonverbal cues. By simply being attentive to the mystery of what God is up to in those around us, we discover the hidden ways that redemption is being woven into the fabric of life. We see it in a conversation with a neighbor or co-worker, by trying to understand the neighborhoods in which we live, and by taking the time to really see the needs God wants to meet.

When we develop the practice of paying attention, we learn to read God's creation to see where he is already at work. We learn to read what is going on in other people. We learn to see needs, yearnings, and hopes. We read the story of others, of neighborhoods, of family members. We read stories that lack good news, and we read stories to see where people are hoping to find good news.

When we pay attention, like when we are reading a good novel, we let the story unfold. We don't work to make it happen. We let it be, and we learn to attend to what's going on. This is what we do when we attend to the world around us. We observe. We listen. We ask questions. We give ourselves time to let everything sink in.

Love pays attention. It offers people an alternative to the distracted, frantic, scattered way of interacting that is so common. When we pay attention, we hear more than words. We hear what's not said. We hear the real story that's being told by others. When we do this in our daily lives, we will find God there, the God of mission, the one who himself sends the Spirit to turn our world around.

For instance, if you frequent a restaurant, offer a prayer for the people who work there every time you enter. Ask God to open your eyes to what he is already doing. Introduce yourself to people who work there and take a few seconds to show genuine interest.

The same approach can be taken with your neighbors or co-workers. Learn their names. Show interest in their lives. The reality is that most people have little interaction with people who are genuinely interested in who they are. Almost always there are some strings attached, some kind of angle.

Perhaps you can start tutoring at a school or get involved with an outreach to street kids or at a nursing home. Go with questions and get to know the people involved. Show interest and listen to their stories. Pay attention, because God is at work somewhere in their lives. Who are some people in your life to whom you could pay attention in a way that demonstrates God's way of paying attention to the world?

*Exegesis* is a fancy word I learned in school that means interpreting the Bible. It means something like deep understanding or critical interpretation. We can approach our neighborhoods the same way. Instead of just going about our lives and not really understanding what's going on in our neighborhoods, we can conduct a neighborhood exegesis to determine what is not obvious. In his wonderful book *God Next Door*, Simon Carey Holt states, "A neighbourhood exegesis means taking a close look at our neighbourhoods, reading them sensitively and critically, understanding and naming them intelligently."[1] Rather than thinking about your neighborhood on a surface level, get a deeper view by seeing four streams of life:

1. What is positive and therefore calls for a response of support (e.g., a local battered-women's home)?
2. What is a natural part of life and therefore calls for redemption and use for God's kingdom (e.g., vacant buildings that resulted from a recession)?
3. What is unacceptable and therefore calls for subversion (e.g., hungry, undocumented families)?
4. What is negative and therefore calls for active resistance (e.g., sex slavery)?

I live in the suburban area of West Houston. On the surface, it looks safe and as though people have their lives together. However, a business called a spa is really a cover for human trafficking and sex slaves. Within a half mile of one of the busiest streets in our area and some five-thousand-square-foot homes sit apartment complexes that house undocumented families who cannot afford to feed their children. Nearby are two buildings owned by a Christian ministry to serve the community with job services, a resale shop, and inexpensive childcare. However, for various reasons, these buildings sit vacant. You can drive past these places and never notice them. I've done so for years. But when you start asking questions about your neighborhood, you may be surprised by what you find.

Where are the places of pain around you? Where are the places of joy and life? What is going on that you don't normally see? Ask the Lord to reveal them to you.

# Part 3 Activity

## An Exegetical Walk[2]

This is an exercise you can do by yourself or with a group. It's a way to see what you don't normally see, to pay attention to what is unspoken.

First, draw a simple map of your neighborhood so you can visualize how it is laid out. Focus on the area where you live that is actually walkable. Set the boundaries of an area that you can walk in a two-hour time frame. Then take a notebook, a pen, and a few of the following questions to help you see what is not obvious.

As you stand outside your residence, look both ways. What do you see? What do you hear or sense? What activities do you notice?

As you walk, notice the architecture of the residences. What is the average age of the buildings? Is there any renovation going on?

What do you notice about the exterior and yards of the residences? Are they cared for?

How many residences are for sale? What indicators of transience do you notice?

Is there a major highway nearby? Imagine how the introduction of this highway changed the neighborhood.

Stop in a quiet spot. Then stop by a busy intersection. What are the smells and sounds of the different places?

How many community or civic buildings are there? What are their purposes? Do they look inviting? Well used?

Is there a local park? What do you notice about it?

What do the design and appearance of the churches in the area communicate to you?

What kinds of commercial buildings are there? Who makes up the clientele?

Are there places where you wouldn't go? Why?

Where are the places of life, hope, and beauty?

What evidence of struggle, despair, neglect, and alienation do you see?

# 17

## Neighbors and Networks

When I think about the question How does God make a difference? the first picture that pops in my mind is the steeple of the church of my childhood. I grew up a mile away from the church my family attended, and I could see the steeple from my bedroom window. I spent more time in that building by the time I was fourteen than in any other building besides my house. That was the place where God-talk happened. It's not that we were ashamed to talk about God outside the building, but when we talked about God working in our world, we focused on getting people to come to the building. All activity of the church was directed toward the center. It might be illustrated this way:

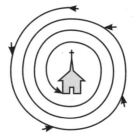

In most cases, this center-focused way of doing church draws a clear line between those who are in and those who are out. Everyone knew who belonged and who did not. Belonging was determined by believing and behaving according to the established patterns of our church. People from the church would go on visitations to meet with people who had not been to church in a while or ever. The visitors would communicate what we were doing at the church and invite them to come to church. We wanted them to belong, but that meant they needed to believe and behave as we did.

Before you assume that I'm speaking against things such as brick-and-mortar churches, sermons, preachers, church leadership, and the like—I make this point because it has become quite popular to trash anything that looks like this—I want you to know that I am *not* against them. I love to preach. I like good sermons. I think we should invite people to join us for Sunday worship. I have served on the staff of a megachurch and have seen the benefits that such a church can offer the world. There is a place for church buildings and for church leadership. I'm not challenging their existence, only the fact that sometimes we limit what God is doing to the church center.

I'd like to present an alternative way based on the force of the church moving out from its center. This way assumes that God works in our centralized church services and events for the sake of the world. It assumes that God is at work—and most of the time more at work—on the fringes in the places that don't look much like church. Of course, God is speaking to our pastors, elders, and church leaders—those with official positions at the center. However, if we think he speaks to those at the center only to bring more people to that center, we are missing what he is doing at the fringes.

This different way of looking at the church recognizes the reality that the Spirit of God works in ways that are outside our control. Visually it could be depicted this way:

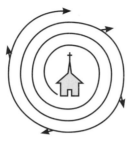

Let's look again at the story of Jesus washing the disciples' feet, this time focusing on another aspect of Jesus's revelation of God and how God works in this other model.

> The evening meal was in progress, . . . so he [Jesus] got up from the meal, took off his outer clothing, and wrapped a towel around his waist. After that, he poured water into a basin and began to wash his disciples' feet, drying them with the towel that was wrapped around him. (John 13:2, 4–5)

Notice the context. This event did not take place at a religious place or in a religious meeting. Jesus ended his time with his disciples over a meal. He lived out his ministry at the intersections of daily life: in homes, at parties, in city streets, at lakeshores. He went where the people were and paid attention to what was going on in people's lives at those places.

Jesus invites us to wash the feet of those around us who may or may not be connected to religious places. We can begin with those who are neighbors and those with whom we network. Our neighbors are those on our streets or in our apartment buildings—as a rule of thumb, those who live within walking distance. Networks include people at work, parents of our kids' friends, family members, and those we know through clubs, civic organizations, local government, and local businesses.

As a way of helping you see what's going on around you, consider the following tic-tac-toe grids, one representing your neighborhood and the other your networks. For your neighborhood, your residence is the center grid. Now write the names of those who live around you. For your networks, put your name in the middle grid. Write the names of those closest to you in your various networks.[1]

Neighbors                              Networks

Where is God at work? He is working in the lives of your neighbors and those in your networks. Your job is to learn to read what God is doing there. Ask God to give you ears to hear what he is doing in their lives and how you might get involved.

# 18

## Going Local

While living in Vancouver, my life was full of Christian work. I served on the staff of a growing church, I studied at a Christian graduate school, and most of my friends were from the church or the school. I had to address the question of how God was going to work through me in specific ways even though I was not rubbing shoulders with people outside the Christian bubble. One of the ways I did this was through drinking coffee. Two blocks from my apartment was a coffee shop that I frequented four or five days a week. There I talked with the owners, interacted with a few friends, and prayed God might change lives. Over a few conversations, Guy, a local business owner, and I became friends. We talked. We shared opinions. We conversed about God. I shared time with him and his wife. And he took me sailing. To see how God was at work, I first looked locally.

For the past few decades, Wendell Berry has been a prophetic voice calling others to a local presence. In his book *The Art of the Commonplace*, he reflects on how early Americans treated the local place where they lived. He writes, "Because they [early Americans] belonged to no place, it was almost inevitable that they should behave violently toward the places they came to. We still have not, in any meaningful way, arrived in America. And in spite of our great reservoir of facts and methods, in comparison to the deep earthly wisdom of established peoples, we still know but little."[1]

According to Berry, the early Americans treated the land violently because they did not respect and belong to the *place*, the land that they took. They consumed *space* for their own benefit. Berry's writings challenge us to slow down and enjoy the place where we live, to enter the rhythms of local life and treat it as part of God's creation.

This requires us to develop a *place spirituality*, as opposed to a *space spirituality*. Most Western church traditions think about God and his activity in this world in spacial terms. We talk about God being present in a nebulous "everywhere" so much that we don't actually encounter him in the local places where we walk and live. God is out there everywhere, somewhere, but we are not sure where. For instance, it is common to hear people say things like, "I will go anywhere God leads me," or "I will minister to anyone who needs it," or "I love *all* people."

This spacial spirituality has been reinforced over the last decade through social networking. We can have all kinds of "friends" on Facebook and thousands of followers on Twitter. We interact in chatrooms, let everyone know about our interests on Pinterest, and spend hours playing games with others while alone with our computers. We make friends in a virtual space that lacks the experience of having a local place.

In contrast, a place spirituality takes seriously the fact that God works through us in specific places. Yes, God wants me to go anywhere he leads, but I am already going on a daily basis to the places where I live now. Yes, God wants me to minister to anyone he brings my way, but will I minister to my neighbor? Yes, God wants me to love all people, but will I love my co-worker who has not treated me well?

How do we begin to step into our local situation and follow God there?

The first step is to observe what's going on in your local place. Shop in stores nearby. Volunteer at a local school. Attend city council meetings. Make yourself visible in your local area by spending time in your front yard or on your porch. Find a local restaurant or coffee shop and become the best customer. While you are doing this, don't assume that you know what needs to happen to make things better. Listen. Seek to understand. Read your neighborhood.

Second, get to know your neighbors. This might sound simple, but be honest. How many of your neighbors on your street can you name? In most situations, we just don't take the time to converse with our neighbors. Excuses abound, and many of them are legitimate. We are too busy. We already have tons of people in our lives. My personal favorite excuse is, "I just don't feel called to invest in my neighbor. It's just not natural for me."

Sometimes we don't like our neighbors because we did not choose them. We live in a world in which we assume we have the right to choose our friends. Dietrich Bonhoeffer opens his bestselling book *Life Together* with these words: "Jesus Christ lived in the midst of his enemies. In the end all his disciples abandoned him. On the cross he was all alone, surrounded by criminals and the jeering crowds. He had come for the express purpose of bringing peace to the enemies of God. So Christians, too, belong not in the seclusion of a cloistered life but in the midst of enemies. There they find their mission, their work."[2] Of course, our neighbors are not our enemies, but often we ignore those who live closest to us.

Shawn is a stay-at-home mom with three kids, one with special needs. Her husband has a high-stress job at a medical implant manufacturer. For a while my wife and I shared life in the same small group that met in their home. Shawn spent time every week talking to her neighbors. She did not do it to save them or recruit them for our church, although she would have been happy if they had found Jesus. She aimed to create a place where people were good neighbors. When we would meet, she always mentioned the various things going on in her neighbors' lives. Because she spent time getting to know her neighbors, she found babysitters, workout partners, and potential friends. These neighborly conversations opened doors for much deeper sharing. One couple shared about marital struggles and another about fears for their children. Because Shawn lived locally, she was able to demonstrate the love of Jesus without forcing it on others.

# 19

## Salt and Light

My grandmother was an incredible cook, that is, if you like things like fried chicken, pot roast, fresh vegetables, and peach cobbler. She lived next door, and I remember fondly walking in her house and seeing the kitchen covered with flour after she had spent the day making pie crusts. However, she had the tendency to overuse salt in her cooking. Then after she put the food on her plate, she would add more salt. Salt brings out the flavor in food, but too much makes even the best food undesirable.

On the other hand, salt that never leaves the saltshaker is of no value. Its value comes when it's added to food. It has no worth by itself. In the Sermon on the Mount, Jesus proclaimed, "You are the salt of the earth. But if the salt loses its saltiness, how can it be made salty again? It is no longer good for anything, except to be thrown out and trampled underfoot" (Matt. 5:13).

Notice how Jesus announces this as fact. Saltiness is part of the identity of his followers. But what exactly does this mean? Now, before you assume that you know what Jesus was talking about because you have heard tons of sermons on this passage, put yourself in the position of those listening to Jesus. First, those listening would know that salt has two functions: adding flavor and food preservation. We emphasize the first today, but they would have used salt for the latter to a greater degree because they did not have refrigerators. Second, Jesus was speaking to Jews, people who would have known the Old Testament very well. They would have understood the covenants between God and the people of Israel. When Jesus spoke of salt, they would have remembered Leviticus 2:13, which speaks of salting the grain offering as a sign of the covenant between God and Israel. And because most people present would have been poor farmers, salting their grain offering would have been a common practice.

Jesus was saying that the people of God are this sign. Like salt, Jesus followers add flavor and preserve the earth. If we cloister ourselves from the world and keep ourselves from rubbing shoulders with our neighbors and networks, we fail to salt the earth. If we force ourselves and our faith on others, we ruin what we are meant to preserve.

The way we are present, scattered like salt, on this earth is how God flavors and preserves the earth. We are a sign, a people who point to a different reality with how we live.

Then Jesus continues: "You are the light of the world. A town built on a hill cannot be hidden. Neither do people light a lamp and put it under a bowl. Instead they put it on its stand, and it gives light to everyone in the house. In the same way, let your light shine before others, that they may see your good deeds and glorify your Father in heaven" (Matt. 5:14–16).

Darkness is the absence of light. When a light is turned on, darkness disperses. Without the people of God, who live in ways that reflect God's love for the world, there is no light. This is not about doing good works or volunteering for every activity possible at church. This is not about trying to live up to some kind of standard of what a good Christian should be. This is about our identity. We are a sign. We ask questions about where we can offer God's love and light to the world. These questions help us pay attention:

- Who is sick, and what kind of care do they need?
- Where is there injustice in our neighborhood? Who are the victims? What kind of advocacy do they need?
- Where are there patterns of racial tension? What kind of racial reconciliation is needed? What kinds of conversations need to happen?
- How are the under-resourced dishonored in our neighborhood? Where are they located? What are their needs? What kinds of friendships are needed to bring honor to them?
- In what ways does the creation of God need tending? How is the environment being harmed? Who are those who tend to God's creation in our neighborhood?
- Who are the forsaken in our neighborhood? Where are the disabled? The orphaned? The addicts? The incarcerated? The elderly?

Marge was our next-door neighbor. She and her brother lived in the apartment next to us. We met her at the pool while our small group was having a cookout. No conversations occurred that suggested she was interested in Jesus. After that we shared a meal or two. Then she was diagnosed with breast cancer. She knew about God and the church. We had not hidden our faith from her. She asked us to pray. We began to walk with her through this time of despair and darkness. She was a single woman of about thirty who had always wanted to get married and have kids, and now before any of that happened, she was losing her hair.

We learned to listen. We learned to pay attention. We learned to be present. We had no answers. What do you say to someone in such darkness? All you can do is be with them and pray that God shines some kind of light of hope.

She made it through. Her hair grew back. She gave her life to Jesus and participated in the life of our church. But the reality is that she was already participating in our life together because we surrounded her first.

After washing the feet of the disciples, Jesus instructed them to do likewise. Then he said, "No servant is greater than his master, nor is a messenger greater than the one who sent him" (John 13:16). Jesus had washed our feet. We were learning to wash each other's feet, and we had the opportunity to wash Marge's feet. In doing so, we were salt and light.

# 20

## Paying Attention to the Routines

I grew up on a family farm. In theory, someone could learn how to run a farm by reading books, listening to experienced farmers, or maybe even getting a degree in agriculture. In reality, the farming life is played out not by following a set of theories or concepts but by living with, responding to, and joining in the mysterious routines of nature. I learned this from my father, grandfather, and uncle, as they taught me the routines of farming. I learned about tending the soil, the timing of planting the crops, the agony of waiting and praying for rain, the anticipation of harvest, and the urgent work of bringing in the crops by living out the story of farming year after year. Even though I have not lived on a farm in twenty-five years, the story of farming is in me because I participated in it.

Making a difference with God is a bit like this. While books, sermons, and concepts about God's love can be helpful, we become difference makers as we listen to God and pay attention to where he is at work in the routines of life. And as we pay attention to these routines, the life of making a difference gets inside of us. It becomes more and more who we are.

On the farm, the work was routine. Every year we did the same things. We plowed, fertilized, planted, waited, and then harvested. Yet in the sameness of those routines, farming was always different. Nature is full of mystery and uncontrollable forces. Farming is about learning to work with the wild mystery of God's creation. Likewise, God's loving mission is wild and mysterious. It's closer than our own skin but so different from us that we don't know how to respond to it.

On the farm, the mystery of nature keeps the farmer humble because he knows he is not in control. The farmer is a lifelong learner because farming is never mastered. Likewise, the way of the difference-making God cannot be mastered; it cannot be controlled. We simply let the story of love enter into our imagination and pay attention to how we can join in.

As we pay attention, we discover that God's way of difference making is different from what we expected. The love of God is nothing else but a revelation. A revelation is something that comes to life from outside our preconceived notions or expectations. No one could come up with something like Jesus, God incarnate, coming to earth and dying on a cross. The revelation of God's work in our world is always a surprise. It's something so mysterious and so good that we don't know what to do with it. While sharing life with those in our neighborhoods and networks, we see that the mysterious goodness of God is found in the routines.

While sitting in a doctor's waiting room waiting for a checkup for one of our four kids, I read an article that said a baby will have his or her diaper changed about thirty-seven hundred times. This means my wife and I changed about fifteen thousand diapers!

Toward the end of our diaper-changing saga, I was preaching about how our mundane choices make a difference, that we can make an impact through ways we assume to be insignificant. While I was preaching, I said something like, "My attitude while changing a diaper makes a difference." This statement was not in my notes. It just came out of my mouth, and I almost had to stop and think about what I was saying. I can choose to have a complaining attitude while serving my children, or I can use this act as a prompter to pray for them.

The routines of small things we do and the attitude we choose to have while doing them can mean the difference between seeing and missing God at work. These routines are not something to get past so that we can get on to the important stuff God wants us to do. They are the routines God wants to redeem. Maybe there are co-workers you avoid. Neighbors who are rude. Family members who don't deserve your attention. A teacher at school who needs encouraging. A coffee barista who feels ignored. God is mysteriously involved in the routines of your encounters with these people. Most of the time we go about the routines of life that are not special and don't seem spiritual, but they are packed with life and mystery. They are filled with the potential to see God at work. We can engage others with self-focus, or we can offer them an attitude of honor, a generous spirit, and the gift of someone who has time for them.

When we pay attention, we open doors for God to move through us wherever we find ourselves, in whatever role we play in life. Then we can see difference makers rise up in all kinds of places:

difference-making moms
difference-making coaches
difference-making mechanics
difference-making janitors
difference-making farmers
difference-making salespersons
difference-making administrators
difference-making waiters

difference-making teachers
difference-making carpenters
difference-making writers
difference-making dads

Take a couple minutes to list three or four of the routines of your life and think about creative ways to redeem them.

# 21

## Paying Attention to Parties

Having a house full of kids has taught me a lot about how God pays attention to people. Children are attracted to fun. They want to be around energy, joy, and laughter. More than anything, they love parties. The four Gospels tell about how kids were drawn to Jesus. They wanted to be with him, even though the disciples tried to push them away. If Jesus had been a religious stuffed shirt who walked around with an air of superiority, children would not have gravitated to him. The same can be said of others who were drawn to him. People liked being with Jesus, except for religious people. All the wrong people from a religious point of view—those on the fringes of first-century society, the poor, the immoral, children, women, and the sick—found themselves enjoying the presence of God.

Paying attention leads us down unexpected paths and to conversations with unusual people. We start hearing and seeing God at work in places we did not expect. Consider this passage:

As Jesus went on from there, he saw a man named Matthew sitting at the tax collector's booth. "Follow me," he told him, and Matthew got up and followed him.

While Jesus was having dinner at Matthew's house, many tax collectors and sinners came and ate with him and his disciples. When the Pharisees saw this, they asked his disciples, "Why does your teacher eat with tax collectors and sinners?"

On hearing this, Jesus said, "It is not the healthy who need a doctor, but the sick. But go and learn what this means: 'I desire mercy, not sacrifice.' For I have not come to call the righteous, but sinners." (Matt. 9:9–13)

I wonder what Jesus saw in Matthew that made him think Matthew would be a good choice to be a part of the Twelve. I wonder if Matthew wondered the same thing. After all, he was at his place of work, which spoke of his allegiance to the Roman government, not the nation of Israel. He was viewed by ardent Jews as an outcast, a traitor, or a "sinner." But Jesus chose Matthew and then ate in his home, along with other tax collectors. This was scandalous. To eat with those people meant that Jesus embraced them and refused to require them to change before he offered them fellowship.

As I reflect on this passage, I wonder about the conversations Jesus shared with this group. I wonder what they said. Did they laugh? Did they tell stories? What did Jesus say to them? If Jesus went in with a religious attitude, he would have been highly purposeful in his conversations and would have steered the talk to some kind of sermonizing. Or maybe he would have presented some kind of "plan of salvation." After all, these people needed to repent.

In cultures like this, a shared meal would have lasted for hours. There would have been lots of stories and conversations. It would have been very normal for Jesus to chime in and add his point of view without having to be intentional or purposeful. All he had to do was engage the people in the room, be present with them, and show interest in them.

Let's take it even further. What if Jesus's participation at Matthew's house focused on listening? What if Jesus didn't preach at all? What if he did not have an agenda except to get to know the people present, to hear where they were coming from, and to see the world through their eyes? What if he actually enjoyed the presence of the people at this party? Is that legitimate ministry?

I learned the power of a party after Eliana came to our small group a few times. She was from Bolivia and had a large family. They would have meals together on all kinds of occasions, and their celebrations usually included salsa dancing. Those were the times when people let their guard down and told stories, shared needs, and revealed who they were.

In my last semester at Texas A & M University, I took a sales class. One of the assignments was to go on sales calls with a local salesperson. I went out with an agricultural pharmaceutical salesman and spent the entire day with him. He did not sell one item that day. He spent most of the time listening, and we spent about three hours helping a rancher herd his cattle into pens and give them their annual vaccinations. Let me reiterate. The salesman did not sell one item. But I noticed how he paid attention to those we called on that day.

In many ways, I'm repulsed by the comparison of gospel ministry to selling pharmaceuticals. However, I saw a man who was actually more interested in engaging people than in selling product. He did not have anything prepackaged to offer. He trusted his ears. Likewise, Jesus's focus lay on the people around him. He met people where they were. He shared life with them. He listened to them. Through this, he became aware of their pain, their hopes, their disappointments, and their needs.

I wonder how our world might change if we did more of this kind of thing. What if we simply shared a meal with a neighbor? Or sat on the porch and talked? Or invited a friend out for coffee? Or took regular walks in the neighborhood and stopped to talk with people who were out? Or learned to throw a party every now and then?

Rebecca met a woman from Africa who still wore her traditional African clothing. While chatting, Rebecca asked her what she missed about life in Africa. She shared her frustration of knocking on her neighbors' doors in America and always hearing, "How can I help you?" like she had to have a purpose for knocking. In her town in Africa, people knock on their neighbor's door just to sit, have a cup of coffee, chat, and be together for a few minutes. She missed spending time with people for no reason.

God shows up when we pay attention like this. Maybe you have a neighbor who is recently widowed and might enjoy a conversation. Or maybe a co-worker has kids who are experimenting with substance abuse. Or maybe the kids down the street lack supervision until late at night. Or . . . Or . . . Or . . .

# Engaging Your World by Reflecting

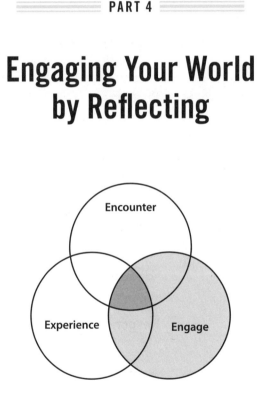

## *Lectio Divina* for Part 4

*Remain in me, as I also remain in you. No branch can bear fruit by itself; it must remain in the vine. Neither can you bear fruit unless you remain in me. I am the vine; you are the branches. If you remain in me and I in you, you will bear much fruit; apart from me you can do nothing. (John 15:4–5)*

**Read**

**Reflect**

**Respond**

**Remain**

# 22

## Reflection

I grew up in a church tradition that emphasized the need to share the message of Jesus and lead people to salvation. The primary point of the church was to invite people into a personal relationship with Jesus Christ so that they could live with him forever. Another church tradition emphasized things such as social justice, racial reconciliation, and financial programs. This tradition focused on ministering to the poor, feeding the hungry, and striving to change social conditions. In the past, it was common for those within these two traditions to judge the other perspective, each assuming that they alone knew the kind of ministry the world needed.

Actually, there are biblical merits for both. Of course God wants those who don't have a relationship with him to repent and turn to him. And if we read our Bibles well, it is painfully obvious that God has an eye toward the poor and the marginalized. Over three hundred verses talk about caring for the poor, the widows, the sick, and other people facing difficult social issues. The problem is that we turn these two views into programs and assume that we know what people need from us, which means that engaging people who need a touch from Jesus involves a predetermined plan as to how to minister to them.

After we pay attention to people, situations, and needs in our local neighborhoods, what do we do next? Just because we see the need does not mean we know how to respond. We cannot boil down God's work in this world to "getting people converted" and/or "social justice." We cannot assume we know what God wants us to do.

Before we had kids, I remember hearing that you cannot raise children in exactly the same way. We have four, and they all require different approaches if we are actually going to engage them and guide them well as parents. While there are some helpful parenting guidelines, following a set of parenting rules turns kids into objects we control, not humans we encounter. When I read the stories about how Jesus engaged people, I see that he never led two people into the kingdom of God the same way. To some he told parables. Others he invited to join him. Others he healed. And to some he gave difficult and challenging words.

There are no recipes for difference making. Before we respond to a need, we must pause, think, listen, and see what God wants to do. We are talking about people and how God wants to relate to people. We are not making widgets or solving math problems. The church is not a business that counts converts and baptisms and numbers of people fed so that it can justify its mission. People are far too complex to be treated as objects. People are prized creations of God, and God invites us to love them by treating them as such.

Treating people as God's prized creations requires an awareness of what God wants to do in their lives. It requires us to develop the habit of hearing God's leading in the midst of a culture that operates as if God does not exist. Now, before you chime in and judge those who don't follow Jesus, you need to realize that the tendency to go through life with a secular point of view invades all of our lives. We live in a disenchanted world, which would have been unfathomable before 1700. With the onset of the scientific age, the world of mystery was explained away by logical analysis that could give a reason and a cause for everything encountered. As a result, we learned how to live as if there is nothing beyond what we can experience with our senses. Mystery, wonder, and being led by God's Spirit became a distant memory.

We are shaped by disenchantment, whether we like it or not. Some long for a return to a premodern way of life. Many are promoting ways of getting back to the first-century church experience as if the culture in which we live does not matter. When we do this, we may very well embrace the mystery of God's leading inside the church, but we fail to integrate it into the rest of life. We do spiritual things that take us out of the world, but when we are sitting in traffic, swinging a hammer, or attending business meetings, those things are outside the realm of our spirituality. None of us wants to admit it, but it is easy to go about life and work completely unaware that God is near, that God is speaking and leading.

Instead of trying to return to a romantic view of what the world used to be like, we need to learn to reflect and hear God's voice in the here and now. This makes me think about a few lines from St. Patrick's morning prayer:

> Christ with me, Christ before me, Christ behind me,
>     Christ in me,
> Christ beneath me, Christ above me,
> Christ on my right, Christ on my left,
> Christ in breadth, Christ in length, Christ in height,
> Christ in the heart of every man who thinks of me,
> Christ in the mouth of every man who speaks of me,
> Christ in every eye that sees me,
> Christ in every ear that hears me.

The final words of Jesus in Matthew, we call them the Great Commission, told the disciples to go and make other disciples and to baptize them in the name of the Father, Son, and Spirit. The specific ways we are to do these things flow out of how Jesus opened and closed the Great Commission. He opened by saying, "All power has been given to me . . ." It's his power that we need to do this. Jesus closed with, "I will be with you always." It's his presence that will direct us.

Reflecting is all about having the humility to know that we don't know how God wants to minister to others. It's about becoming aware of God's presence around us and getting in touch with what the Spirit of God is already doing. There are no recipes for this kind of mission in our world.

# 23

## Listen Up

After we have paid attention, reflecting on what God wants to do requires prayer. However, prayer sounds so formal, so religious. It's something many people do at the beginning of the day so that they can go about the rest of their lives. Henri Nouwen is one writer who has opened my eyes to a conversational way of praying about making a difference. He wrote, "To pray, therefore, is to connect whatever human struggle or pain we encounter—whether starvation, torture, displacement of peoples, or any form of physical and mental anguish—with the gentle and humble heart of Jesus. . . . Prayer is the way to become and remain part of Jesus's mission to draw all people to the intimacy of God's love."[1]

In the teaching that followed Jesus's washing of feet, Jesus taught his disciples, "Remain in me, as I also remain in you. No branch can bear fruit by itself; it must remain in the vine. Neither can you bear fruit unless you remain in me. I am the vine; you are the branches. If you remain in me and I in you, you will bear much fruit; apart from me you can do nothing" (John 15:4–5).

We bear difference-making fruit when we are connected to God. Action alone is a good thing, but it's not God's fruit. Of course, action is required for mission. Faith without deeds is not faith, after all. We need God's eyes to see the needs around us. We need God's compassion to feel the pain that we see. We need God's love for people so that we will consider them more important than ourselves. We need God's power to do something about the needs. We need God's voice so that we act with wisdom. But we are not offering God to others unless our deeds come out of prayer.

Prayer opens the door for entry into mission. Prayer is waiting on God. Prayer is coming before him with all that would hinder us from being bearers of his love. Prayer is a means for formation so that we can be God's light in the midst of the darkness. Prayer makes us into the kind of people who embody impact that is actually God's impact.

God's direction to his people seems to vary quite radically from one situation to the next. His counsel never looks the same twice. In fact, the Bible contains quite a few stories in which God's people made assumptions about how God works and it led to massive failure. One example is the battle of Ai (Joshua 7). After the miraculous and overwhelming victory at Jericho, Joshua led the people to Ai. Instead of seeking God's direction, Joshua made all kinds of assumptions about what it would take to defeat Ai. The Israelites were soundly defeated.

God sees what we cannot. Even though that's an obvious statement, we too often act as if we have God's point of view. We see a need and jump in with both feet. Many times, I've observed a need, and the Lord has given me compassion for the situation. But I haven't always responded in the best way. One time I had a huge concern for a person, and he told me over coffee, "If you have a concern about my life, please tell me." I thought, *Wow! What a wide-open door.* So I jumped in with words that were met with great resistance. At first I just blamed his hard heart, but after some time had passed, I realized that my words were judgmental and condemning.

Instead of taking advantage of the moment, I wish I had reflected on what God was saying. If I had, I would have paused and then sought to understand more about where my friend was coming from. He was not looking for me to tell him about any concerns I had about his life. In fact, I think he may have been testing me to see if I would judge him. I could have responded in many different ways that day. But I did not reflect before I acted.

One of the reasons I included the *lectio divina* process for reading the Bible in this book is to prepare us to reflect before acting. Those of you who are extroverted activists may feel this does not fit your personality. You may be more inclined to get out and just do stuff to make a difference. Reflecting, if done well, will lead to action, but it will be action that is more likely shaped by God's guidance. *Lectio divina* shapes our imagination to hear God in a way that lines up with the Scriptures. It takes us inside the Scriptures to see the character of God, who makes a difference. It reshapes our character so that we can hear God rightly, and it provides creative ways to respond that go beyond our logical responses.[2]

Sue has shown me a way of reflecting that points us in the right direction. She is a quiet, unassuming retired secretary. A couple years ago she had a car accident with a neighbor. After they exchanged insurance information, she went home stressing about the fact that she had hit someone's car. Then she sensed something she did not expect. She felt compelled to go and tell her neighbor about Jesus's love for him. She timidly knocked on his door and asked if she could tell him about how Jesus had changed her life. He listened and responded. He turned his life around. His wife later told Sue that until that point he had never been open to hearing about Jesus.

God's guidance is present. Are you listening?

Take a few minutes now to pray for some of the people you listed at the end of chapter 17. Ask the Lord to speak to you about how he is working in their lives and what you should or shouldn't do to help further his plans.

# 24

## Praying beyond the Need

After we observe our world by paying attention, we pray about what we see and feel. We pray for the things that are on our hearts as we relate to people. We might pray for God to help a student we are tutoring. We might ask for a neighbor to see their need for Jesus. We might ask for God to help a co-worker who's recently lost his wife to deal with his grief. We offer prayers about the obvious needs we observe in the world around us.

In addition to praying for the needs that are clear, we also need to pray in ways that take us beyond what is immediately obvious. Need-driven prayers are great, but they can limit us to what we want to see happen, and thereby we may miss what God wants to do at a deeper level.

My friend Jake and his wife want to see God work in them to impact those who live near them. Recently, he started a small group that meets in his house, and it is comprised of people who live near him and want to see God change the world around them. He also has a non-Christian friend named Janet whose passion in life is to rescue abused and abandoned pets, specifically dogs. It just so happens that this is a significant problem in their neighborhood, and most of the people in the group are dog lovers. They have befriended this woman over meals, and now they are rallying around her passion.

Jake offers prayers that relate to the need of dealing with the social issue of the dogs. He also prays that Janet will become open to the gospel. But he does not stop there. He also prays that God might open him up to new ways of relating to Janet and rescuing dogs.

There are a couple of practical ways to do this. First, pray through the Lord's Prayer in a way that moves beyond simply repeating memorized words. Take each line of the Lord's Prayer and add your own words to it, keeping in mind those in your neighborhoods and networks. Doing so might look something like this:

*"Our Father . . ."*
Thank you, Lord, that you are my Father, that you are the loving Father who wants to transform me and those around me. Father, give me your heart for my co-workers. Honestly, I don't like _____ that much, but she needs a touch from you. Change my heart of judgment.

Reveal your heart to _____. Help her to see you for who you are.

*"who is in heaven . . ."*
God, you are above the world. You are beyond what I can see and feel. Reveal yourself to me. Show me your point of view so that I can get involved in your work.

*"hallowed be your name . . ."*
You are worthy, great, and glorious. Thank you for who you are. Make your name great in my workplace too. May you be glorified.

"Your kingdom come, your will be done on earth as it is in heaven" lies at the crux of this prayer. Praying these words shifts our mind-set from praying about needs to praying for God's restoration of creation, the manifestation of the kingdom of God here on earth. When we pray for the kingdom to come, we offer up the alcoholic neighbor, we cry out for battered women, we call out on behalf of the immigrant families who don't have enough to eat but can't get help because they fear deportation. We operate under the assumption that every prayer we offer changes the world in some way. We may not see how it does, but we trust that the prayer for the coming of the kingdom opens a door for God to do something that would not have happened without that prayer.

This pattern of praying is something you might do alone in a time set apart for God each day. Such a prayer will allow your imagination to be shaped by what God wants to do in our world and will tune in your spirit with what the Spirit is already doing. The key to doing this is to begin doing it. Don't make grandiose commitments or set huge goals of praying for thirty to forty-five minutes per day. Just begin doing it.

Let me suggest this. Over the next day or two, set aside fifteen minutes. Maybe you get up fifteen minutes earlier, turn off the TV for fifteen minutes, or take fifteen minutes during your lunch break. Find a place where you won't be interrupted. It could be a quiet place in your house. For some, going for a walk helps. For others, sitting alone in their car is a good place to be alone. Then get comfortable. Perhaps put on some quiet background music or light a candle. Then begin by simply asking God to enliven your prayers, to teach you to pray. Walk through each phrase of the Lord's Prayer. Don't force it. Just offer to God whatever is on your heart. Push away any thoughts that your prayers are not adequate. Talk with God with the knowledge that you are fully loved by God and embraced by him. In that moment, you have God's full attention. After you speak to God, pause and listen. See

if God wants to put something on your heart that goes beyond what you are saying. If you get done before the fifteen
minutes is up, just sit with God quietly.

After you pray, share your experience with a friend and
talk about how you feel about doing this more.

# 25

## Praying in the Moments

A few years ago, I picked up an anonymously written book titled *The Way of the Pilgrim*. The author was a Russian Orthodox monk from the fourteenth century. I'm not sure why I picked it up, because reading books like this was not my norm. However, I was intrigued by the autobiographical story about this peasant monk who repeated the Jesus Prayer as many times per day as possible until it became so natural for him to pray that he reached a point of continual awareness of God's presence. The prayer goes like this: "Lord Jesus Christ, Son of God, have mercy on me, a sinner." He prayed this until it became as natural to him as breathing. Some call this kind of praying "breath prayers."[1]

I was drawn to this, but I was also concerned. I did not want to pray in "vain repetition," as the King James Version translates words in Matthew 6:7, where Jesus instructs his disciples not to babble on like the pagans. Somewhere I had heard that repeating a sentence or phrase like this was nothing but babbling on to get God's attention.

However, the repetition of the Jesus Prayer has a different purpose: that of training our attention. It's like when I was learning to play baseball as a kid. Because I loved the game and I wanted to play well, I carried a ball with me. Or if I didn't have a ball, I was looking for a rock to throw. If I did not have either, I would go through the motions of throwing a ball as I walked. This became so natural that I would do it without thinking.

I'm not yet as consistent at breath prayer as I was at tossing a baseball. I'm growing into it, and the more I do it, the more aware I become of God around me. I see its benefit. So each morning, I wake and slowly whisper, "Lord Jesus Christ, Son of God, have mercy on me, a sinner." Even if chaos quickly consumes our house with all the commotion of getting kids ready for school, I can use this simple prayer to focus my heart, calm my emotions, and keep my mind focused on the One who surrounds me with his love.

In his book *Bringing the Church to the World*, N. T. Wright writes about praying difference making into reality. He introduces the breath prayer as revealed in *The Way of the Pilgrim*, and then he expands on it. He challenges us to move from calling on Jesus to encounter the persons of the Trinity. Focusing only on Jesus can turn us inward and cause us to think only of what God is doing within us as individuals. Wright offers a way to open our hearts to what the Father and the Spirit are doing in the world. He suggests this:

> Father almighty, maker of heaven and earth:
> Set up your kingdom in our midst
> Lord Jesus Christ, Son of God:
> Have mercy on me a sinner.
> Holy Spirit, breath of God:
> Renew me and all the world.[2]

There is power in praying this way. It invites God to work inside of us as individuals, while at the same time it opens our eyes to God's larger work all around us. However, it is ambitious to make these three stanzas a regular breath prayer. One of the best ways to make this prayer a part of your life is to find something you repeat often during the day and use that as a trigger to say this prayer. I do this with my phone. The act of opening my phone prompts me to pray this prayer. I don't pray it as much as I breathe, but I have made the prayer a bigger part of my life.

What could you use as a trigger to prompt you to offer up this simple prayer?

# 26

## Reflecting Together

When I lived in Vancouver, during the warmer months of the year, I would walk around downtown, and I'd often stop to watch an impressive sight. A chess master would set up chessboards and invite passersby to play him, up to twenty-four simultaneously. It was fascinating to watch this solitary expert move from board to board, eliminating his competition.

Sometimes the call to hear God's direction feels like a call to be a solitary prayer master, one who stands alone trying to move the right pieces so differences can be made. All of the pressure falls on us to see the need and then to seek God for a solution. So we try and try. We pray for the kingdom to come. We reflect and seek God for his direction. But no matter how hard we work at it, our private prayers and our private efforts don't measure up to our expectations.

Often the source of the frustration is not personal weakness but unrealistic expectations. We assume that hearing God is first and foremost something we do as individuals and only secondarily something we do together. In reality, it may very well be the other way around.

We do have an issue that stands in the way of this. It's called Western individualism. For the last three hundred years or so in the West (that includes Europe, Canada, the United States, Australia, and New Zealand), we have bought into a cultural perspective that the isolated individual is the core of personal identity. Put in simple terms, our self-identity is rooted in how we view ourselves. Philosophers, psychologists, and pop-culture icons have shaped this perspective. One philosopher got this individualistic ball rolling by founding personal existence on the fact that humans are thinking beings. His famous statement is "I think, therefore I am."

Others have built on this idea of the self throughout the last few centuries. Some have taught us that we are feeling beings (I feel, therefore I am), sexual beings (I have desires, therefore I am), and working beings (I work, therefore I am). The opinions about the essence of an individual vary, but there is one thing that remains constant: the focus on "I." The "I," the grand individual, is the glowing sun around which all else revolves.

This idea impacts how we talk about our relationship with God. We talk about having a personal relationship with God or relating to God as if no one else in the world exists. We might say something like, "I pray, therefore I am." Or when we talk about hearing God's direction, for ourselves or others who need him, we assume this is a solitary act.

The Bible was written in a different time and with a different idea about personal identity. The English language can make it difficult to see this corporate identity point of view. In English, the word *you* can be either plural or singular. Because we think about our personal relationship with God first, and we are taught to read the Bible as a part of our private times of prayer, we miss the fact that most of the time when the word *you* is used in the Bible, it is referring to a group, a church, or a nation of people. Here is one example:

> I always thank my God for you because of his grace given you in Christ Jesus. For in him you have been enriched in every way—with all kinds of speech and with all knowledge— God thus confirming our testimony about Christ among you. Therefore you do not lack any spiritual gift as you eagerly wait for our Lord Jesus Christ to be revealed. He will also keep you firm to the end, so that you will be blameless on the day of our Lord Jesus Christ. God is faithful, who has called you into fellowship with his Son, Jesus Christ our Lord. (1 Cor. 1:4–9)

When Paul wrote, "You do not lack any spiritual gift," he was not writing to an individual. The word *you* is plural. No individual has all of the gifts. He was speaking to a group of people who were experiencing the presence of Christ, as he stated "Christ among you [plural]."

I don't have to listen to God's direction by myself. This is why praying with other Christians for our neighbors and networks can be very powerful. For instance, in chapter 17, you listed a few people in your neighborhood and networks who need an experience of God's love. What if you shared two of those names with a few other people—maybe a small group or Sunday school class—and asked them to pray with you? Then see how God might speak through that experience. We need each other. Our community efforts strengthen our private efforts, and our private efforts feed our community life.

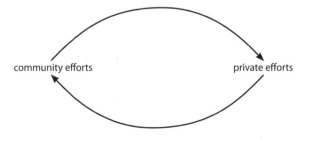

community efforts          private efforts

You don't have to figure out how to make a difference alone. Find a small group or volunteer in a ministry. Join a discipleship class or a recovery group. Go on a mission trip or find a place to serve the community. Rub shoulders with other Christians.

# 27

# Community That Hears God

I hope you are reading this book with at least one other person or a small group. While you can benefit greatly by reading a book alone, when you are able to discuss it with others, that benefit is multiplied. That being said, often when people gather to discuss a book like this, they develop habits, and sometimes those habits turn into ruts. For instance, people arrive at a home for a small group and engage in small talk. Then the leader calls everyone to attention and leads the group in the discussion. Then someone closes in prayer. There's nothing wrong with this pattern; it's just that too many times there's so little variation to it. It's just what a group does. We do it without questioning it. If God were to show up and invite us to do something else, we'd miss his voice.

James 5:16 says, "The prayer of a righteous person is powerful and effective." We need each other as we pray, and thereby we are changed, growing in righteousness and power. However, so many people meet every week as "functional atheists." We operate our groups as if God were not really present. But you might respond, "Well, our group worships every week." That's great, but don't you want more than singing a few songs and then moving on to the next part of the meeting? Jesus said, "Where two or three gather in my name, there am I with them" (Matt. 18:20). I am all for worship, Bible discussion, and prayer. They will make your group better. But doing them as activities is a poor substitute for actually meeting with God as a group.

One of the best ways to increase an expectation of meeting with God is to break up the routine. Do something different when you meet with your group of prayer friends. Change the order of activities. Insert something different into the mix. Meet outside. Change the arrangement of the chairs. Don't do the DVD study for a week and instead have some time of quiet reflection.

You may think it is the job of the small group leader to think about such things, but in reality, every group member is responsible to come prepared to hear God in the meeting. If you are stuck in a rut and put rut-like expectations upon the leader to do what he or she always does, then when there is a change and God does speak, you won't be ready for it. What if God wants to speak to you about how the group might minister to a friend in need? What if the Spirit wants to lead you in the way the group should pray for the neighborhood? What if the presence of Jesus comes to you with a specific Scripture passage to share with the group? Will you be prepared for it?

Our neighborhoods and networks need more than good Bible studies. They need gatherings of people who will embody the love and presence of Jesus. This doesn't look the same from group to group. What happens in one group cannot be reproduced in another because God is dynamic and so is everyone else in your group, whether it's just two or three of you meeting in a coffee shop on Saturday mornings or twenty of you meeting in a home on Thursday evenings. We need all of these different kinds of groups to hear God and respond to his leading to make a difference.

Here are some practical ways to break out of a rut and invite God's leading in your group:

1. Seek God's presence in your group meetings. Bible studies are good, but if you focus on Bible information and not on God's living presence, then you are settling for less than the best. When you meet, expect to meet with God, not just the people who show up.

2. Join forces with two or three others to pray in a specific way. If you commit to praying through the Lord's Prayer, you will be much more successful at it if you have a couple friends who will do the same. You might even get together and talk about it from time to time.

3. Use a group meeting to talk about some of the people you know who need a touch of God's love. Maybe it's a neighbor whose husband just lost his job, or a co-worker who has lost hope, or a kid you've met at the school who goes home to an empty house every evening, or a woman you talk to at the nursing home, or a single mom at the apartment complex. Make a list of these people.

4. Ask God about how you as a group can pray for the people on the list. Start off by spending some time in worship. Listen to God's leading about how the group could be a blessing to someone on the list.

5. Pray that God will open doors to demonstrate more about how the group relates to God. For instance, host a cookout and invite some of the people on the list.

6. Go on a prayer walk together. (See the activity box below.)

## Part 4 Activity

### Prayer Walk

One of the best ways to break out of the small group rut is to do something totally different. Instead of having a normal group meeting, go on a prayer walk together. This is simply a concrete way to practice intercessory prayer for a specific neighborhood. By walking through a neighborhood and praying together, you can invite God to bless people and touch their lives while becoming aware of the ways that God wants the group or individuals to respond to their needs. Often it can be helpful to do this with the neighborhood exegesis in mind (see chap. 16).

Some might think that such an activity is only for the superspiritual, but that need not be the case. The following guidelines will help anyone pray while walking:

- Set a time for the prayer walk for about thirty minutes.
- Walk in groups of two or three in a specific neighborhood where you want to see God move in a greater way.
- If you are comfortable with praying aloud as you walk, feel free to do so. If not, then pray silently and talk about your prayers. However, do not call attention to yourselves.
- If someone asks what you are doing, respond, "We're praying that God would bless this neighborhood. Is there any special way we can pray for you?"
- Although it is not the primary purpose of prayer walking, be open to opportunities to interact with and bless people who arise out of your experience.
- Afterward, gather to share your prayers, observations, and experiences. What did you learn about the neighborhood? How was God manifest in this experience?

# 28

## Prayer and Fasting

Once there was a boy who could not speak. At times, he would lose control of his body in a kind of fit. When this would happen, he would foam at the mouth, grind his teeth, and even roll into a fire or a body of water. Today, this condition might be diagnosed as something like epilepsy, but before modern medicine, people often attributed such conditions to the work of demons.

We read about this story in the Gospel of Mark. There we are told that the disciples of Jesus were asked to help the boy, but they could not. Jesus, who had been praying, went to the boy and cast out the unclean spirit, saying, "You deaf and mute spirit, I command you, come out of him and never enter him again." Afterward, the disciples asked why they were not successful. Jesus said, "This kind can come out only by prayer" (Mark 9:29). Some ancient manuscripts add the words "and fasting." The disciples tried to help the boy in their own power and efforts. Their intentions were good, but they lacked the faith that would have given them the ability to be of benefit to the boy.

Making a difference is a call to war, but it's not the kind of war we might imagine. Difference makers understand the invisible nature of this war. This is a battle between darkness and light, between redemption and chaos, between patterns of sin and patterns of love. The New Testament assumes this point of view. The apostle John wrote, "The one who does what is sinful is of the devil, because the devil has been sinning from the beginning. The reason the Son of God appeared was to destroy the devil's work" (1 John 3:8). In our world, we often don't think this way. We see poor people; we send them to the welfare office. We see sick people; we call a doctor. We see hunger; we suggest a food pantry.

The disciples did not possess the character of faith to be an answer for the boy. When Jesus first heard about how they could not help him, he responded, "You unbelieving generation, . . . how long shall I stay with you? How long shall I put up with you? Bring the boy to me" (Mark 9:19). They had yet to allow themselves to be shaped by the hand of God in such a way that they would be ready with faith to respond to the needs at hand.

The apostle Paul put it this way: "Put on the full armor of God, so that you can take your stand against the devil's schemes. For our struggle is not against flesh and blood, but against the rulers, against the authorities, against the powers of this dark world and against the spiritual forces of evil in the heavenly realms" (Eph. 6:11–12).

How do we put on this armor for this war in our modern world, where talk about a spiritual realm and unseen influences is called into question? The greatest trap of Satan in our world is convincing us that nothing exists beyond what we can apprehend with our five senses. These key principles will help us understand the war we face:

1. The spiritual realm is real. We don't often think about this in our everyday lives, but there are such things as demons, angels, and a realm where a form of warfare

transpires. If we fail to see this, the enemy has already won.

2. There is an enemy. His name is Satan, and he has demons who are former angels who wage war against the aims of God and his creation.

3. This enemy works through the principalities and powers. These are patterns of the world that are evil and produce ways of life that undermine love. Such patterns include generational poverty, workaholic lifestyles, consumerist spending, and much more. These patterns of our culture are so established that we rarely even question their existence. Not all of them undermine God's love, but many of them do.

4. This enemy works against us personally and in our relationships. The enemy seeks to establish life patterns that are destructive in people. These range from those that are obvious, such as substance abuse, to the covert, such as gluttony or debt. Ultimately, the enemy works to drive wedges between people and between people and God.

5. The enemy uses strongholds in the mind, which are thought patterns that do not line up with God's ways. The primary tool at Satan's disposal is lying. If he can get humans to believe that a lie is the truth, then his war efforts can be easily advanced. For instance, if Satan can get a husband to believe the lie that his wife must make him happy or he has the right to find happiness elsewhere, then he can undermine covenantal love in marriage. If he can get us to believe that God is vengeful, controlling, and looks on us with displeasure, then he can drive us away from the reality of God's love.

God fights for us in ways we can't, don't, or won't. Making a difference is rooted in the action of God, who never stops coming against the lies we so easily believe. The mission of

God's people is to put themselves on the line between the revelation of God's love and those in need of that love.

We put ourselves in this place through prayer. We see the war for what it is. We know we cannot make things right without tapping into what we cannot see. For a neighbor experiencing domestic violence, we pray. For a co-worker who's angry with God, we pray. For a family down the street who cannot afford to feed their kids, we pray. We pray not as an alternative to doing something; we pray so that we might have the power to step in with more than good ideas or what we think they need. We pray so that we might act in God's power and make a difference beyond logical answers.

What are some ways you can pray that your eyes might be opened to the spiritual warfare that is transpiring?

# Engaging Your World by Acting

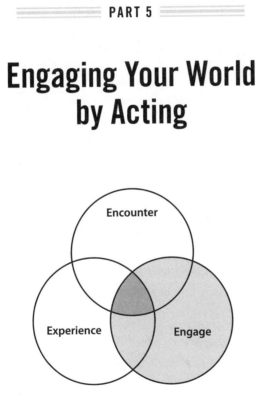

*Greater love has no one than this: to lay down one's life for one's friends. You are my friends if you do what I command. I no longer call you servants, because a servant does not know his master's business. Instead, I have called you friends, for everything that I learned from my Father I have made known to you. You did not choose me, but I chose you and appointed you so that you might go and bear fruit—fruit that will last—and so that whatever you ask in my name the Father will give you. (John 15:13–16)*

**Read**

**Reflect**

**Respond**

**Remain**

# 29

## The Action of Improv

Years ago, I played one of the brothers in a local production of the musical *Joseph and the Amazing Technicolor Dreamcoat*. I loved it when the director pointed to us and yelled, "Action!" At that point, all of the unseen preparatory work—prop construction, costume sewing, line memorization, vocal practices, dance rehearsals—became visible. Action meant we could enjoy the benefits of our labors.

Difference makers act. They do something that is visible and concrete, something that builds on the unseen acts of paying attention and reflecting. Now the visible action comes to light. The concrete responses to the needs rise to the top.

I once heard Eugene Peterson say something like, "The most spiritual thing to do might be simply changing your wife's tire on her car." These simple words tore down the pomp and circumstance of ambitious dreams about Christian ministry for me. When I heard them, I was a young man looking for ways to do something great for God. I wanted some kind of script that would show me what to do. I secretly hoped that the great pastor and Bible translator could point me in the right direction. He could show me how to respond with actions that would make a difference in the world. I didn't get what I was expecting. Is it possible that changing my wife's tire might be the most significant thing I can do on any given day?

The Bible speaks of the Son as the Word of God and the Spirit as the Wisdom of God. The Son and the Spirit have come and continue to come without a fixed script. When Jesus arrived on the scene, his actions blew away all the scripts that people had for God's Messiah. They thought he would come as a king who would set up a rule of power, but instead he came with the power of a self-sacrificial love that led him to the cross.

Then when the Spirit came, so many of the scripts about how God works were thrown out. For instance, Peter expected the work of the Spirit to focus on the Jewish people (see Acts 10). But the Samaritans were converted and filled with the Spirit. The Gentiles likewise. No one expected God to move the way God moved.

When it comes to responding faithfully to the needs we see in our neighborhoods and networks, I think most people are like me. We want scripts. We want a plan that will work. Give me some lines to memorize so that I can know how to talk to people the right way. Give me the steps so that I can do the right thing to bless people in need. Faithful response is not about getting our lines right. Faithful response is about being present in the moment and responding appropriately.

This reminds me of *Whose Line Is It Anyway?*, a TV show that consisted of a panel of four actors who created characters, short scenes, and songs on the spot. They would improvise and play off one another in response to situations and scenarios presented to them by the host. Improv acting like this requires participants to focus in the moment so they can faithfully respond to the situation and the characters created by the other performers.[1]

Jesus calls us to wash the feet of others. The specific ways we respond to the needs of the world and wash people's feet depend on our ability to improvise. We read the needs in our neighborhoods and networks. We reflect by taking these needs and situations to the Lord to see how the Spirit is leading, and then we respond appropriately.

So what does improvisational response look like? In its simplest form, it looks like God with skin coming to people in a way that reflects how God came to the world in Jesus Christ. Dallas Willard writes about this by saying, "No means of communication between God and us is more commonly used in the Bible or the history of the church than the voice of a definite, individual human being."[2] God came through Jesus by expressing love that was fully displayed on the cross. Jesus expressed his love in total self-sacrifice. "No servant is greater than his master, nor is a messenger greater than the one who sent him" (John 13:16). These were Jesus's words right after he washed the disciples' feet. To be God with skin means that we go as servants to the world.

If we allow this rule of love to shape our lives, then our response of improvisation will be an expression of love. For some, it will be a significant response, like adopting a child, inviting a homeless family to live with them, or addressing an obvious social need. My wife, Shawna, was adopted at thirteen by James and Suzanne Bell. They embraced improv by responding to a girl who was trying to get away from a life that was harsh and cruel. They did not take this response lightly, because they saw it as an investment in someone's life. Today, Shawna is the incredible mother of four and a pastor and speaker who invests in others.

Your improv need not be so dramatic. Maybe for you, it's changing a diaper and singing over your child. Maybe it's being a blessing to your spouse, who has had an incredibly stress-filled week. Maybe it's a conversation over the fence with a neighbor. Maybe it's going for a walk with a friend who needs your support. If we are not faithful to extend God's hands of love in the small things, how can we be faithful to do so in the things that seem bigger?

Being God with skin is not just about having the right words or quoting the right Scripture passage. It's about learning to be there for each other. One family I know regularly visits a local apartment complex where many poor, unregistered immigrants live. They bring their kids, who are in elementary and middle school. Their kids play kickball with the children in the apartments. They help them with their homework. The families share meals together. In other words, they allow loving relationships to be improvised, wherever that improvisation might lead them.

# Part 5 Activity

**How Will You Act?**

Review the list below of ways that you might visibly act to make a difference. Pray over it. See what grabs you. Then meet with a friend and/or a small group to discuss what you are feeling compelled to do. See if another person feels a similar compulsion or if someone might join you. Then make a plan to do it. After you do it, sit down with your friend or your small group and talk about how it went. Here are some questions to guide the conversation: What did you enjoy? What was the most challenging? How did you sense God moving? What would you do differently? What's next?

- Throw a party at your house or in a neighborhood clubhouse and invite your neighbors.
- Host a coffee and dessert night.
- Lead a food drive or coat drive and ask the neighbors if they want to participate.
- Participate in homeowners' association meetings.
- Start an exercise group in the neighborhood.
- Lead a book group and invite neighbors to suggest books they might want to read.
- Throw a block party.
- Use a unique skill or gift to bless others. For instance, if you like working on cars, have an oil-change day. Or if you enjoy baking, host a cooking class.
- Mow the yard or weed the garden of a neighbor.
- Purchase some extra groceries and drop them by the home of a neighbor who needs some extra food.
- Borrow a tool or a cup of sugar from a neighbor. One way to tear down walls in a relationship is to allow others to bless you. It puts them at ease.

# 30

## Bad Improv

When I was in my early twenties, I got a call from Bob, a childhood friend. He and his wife were in town for a conference, and they wanted to buy me lunch. After we got caught up, the reason for the lunch became obvious. For the next hour, I sat through a multilevel marketing presentation, and all the while I was boiling inside. The only thought going through my mind was, *I'm giving up the Dallas Cowboy football game for this*. I wish I had had the guts to walk out of the restaurant mid-sentence.

This experience made me think about Eli, the owner of a restaurant our small group frequented. We would sit with him and his family long after our meals, talking and drinking coffee. Over time, we developed a friendship with Eli, so much so that he invited a couple of us to go fishing with him in Galveston. After failing to catch anything, the three of us went to lunch. While eating shrimp, Trey (a guy from the group) proceeded to tell Eli all about Jesus. Obviously, Eli was not interested in the conversation, but Trey continued on. And the more Trey talked, the more Eli squirmed. I wanted to reach over and pull Trey's tongue out, but I did not trust my instincts. Since Trey had mentored me previously, I assumed he knew something I did not. Unfortunately, that encounter really messed up our friendship with Eli. Subsequent conversations with him were always met with resistance. I wonder if Eli felt the same way I did while enduring the marketing presentation.

After years of reflecting on that experience, I now see how Eli was our evangelism target. We had been taught to befriend people, share Jesus with them, and to recruit them to participate in our small group. Of course, no one put it in such crass terms, but the reality is that we treated Eli as a project, not as a person.

We did a lot right. We paid attention to the situation. We reflected by praying for Eli. We hung out with Eli and his family at the restaurant. We did not try to force Jesus down his throat and then move on. We invested time in that relationship. However, we needed a more loving way to act than giving the canned sales pitch for Jesus. Were we genuinely interested in Eli, his questions, his life, and his fears, or were we just interested in getting him to pray a prayer? We never dreamed that God might already be working in Eli's life in some way and that our job was to listen to Eli and the Spirit to see what was already happening. We assumed that we had to take God to Eli. In the process, we were practicing bad improv.

A couple years ago, Shawna and I participated in a small group with people from various social and economic experiences. There were three or four adults who had been raised in generational poverty. One person had been in jail multiple times but now was serving God. Another had lost his business during a recession and now was homeless and unhirable because he was "overqualified." Three or four others came from a middle-class background.

Our topic of conversation was the biblical call to minister to "the poor," those entrapped for a variety of reasons in patterns that keep them mired in poverty. Those conversations were some of the richest I've ever had. The assumption of the book we were reading together was that those with money should minister to those who do not have any, that it is a one-way ministry. Because our group was made up of people from various economic experiences, we had open conversations about this one-way perspective.

Here is a peek into some of what was shared. "This book calls people 'the poor,' but I don't see myself as part of 'the poor.' We don't sit on our porches in the inner city talking about how poor we are." In other words, the language labeled them and objectified them. I will never forget when one person said, "We don't want your money. If all you want to do is give us money, keep it. If you are interested in interacting with us by learning and talking, then you will find no resistance to that." In a similar vein, another person stated, "I have no desire to own a home or become middle-class." He made enough money and didn't want the "good" life, which he viewed as a rat race filled with stress and unnecessary pressure.

Through these conversations, I realized that effective improv means we don't minister to "the poor." Instead, it strips away the "us and them" mentality and embraces a "with" mentality. It's not a one-way flow of ministry. In fact, every time I minister to someone who needs Christ's love, Christ ministers to me through them at least as much as I minister to them, as long as I have the humility to listen. But this is what friends do. Friends treat one another with mutuality and give space for reciprocity. Effective improv makes room for improvisational learning and journeying together.

Very often, good improv comes not in what we have to tell people but in questions that seek to create more conversations. As opposed to telling people what they should think or how they should believe or how they need to change their behavior, we need to develop an ability to respond with questions. For instance, in a conversation with someone who is convinced that all roads lead to God, instead of debating that point of view, why not respond with questions? For instance, a conversation might go:

> Friend: I cannot commit to one religion because I think all religions lead to God.
>
> Christ follower: Why do you think that way?
>
> Friend: I cannot believe in a God who allows all the pain in the world. So we have to find our own way.
>
> Christ follower: Why do you assume that God causes or allows all the pain in the world?
>
> Friend: I was taught that God is all-powerful and can do whatever he wants. I just cannot believe that anymore.
>
> Christ follower: So when you think about God, what do you picture in your head?

In other words, we should respond with questions that might open doors to conversations, demonstrating that we really care what people think, as opposed to trying to convince them that they are wrong and we are right.

Write out a few questions you could use in a conversation with a friend to better understand his or her point of view about God.

# 31

## Inclusive Improv

A few years ago, I was in a small group with a college student named Jenny. Her friend Stephanie was a committed agnostic. She was a national merit scholar who had grown up in a nominally Catholic family and had no desire to talk about Jesus. Since she liked Jenny, she would join us for meals, and we all became good friends. Her comment to us one night was, "You guys actually have fun. What's up with you?" Over time, she started asking questions and eventually came to a small group meeting.

When Stephanie returned for the fall term, she started going to church and was involved in a small group. One night, the small group broke into groups of three to pray. Someone felt led to ask her if she had ever prayed to commit her life in a formal way to Jesus. At that point she had not, but she said she was ready.

We engaged Stephanie by inviting her to belong as a friend. We included her in our life together without any expectation that she would have to line up with our thinking. As she started to feel like she belonged, she asked how she could participate in what we were doing. She started behaving as a disciple even before she officially became one. Then she confessed her belief in Christ. We were practicing inclusive improv. She was invited into the action from the beginning. The normal pattern for inviting people into a relationship with Jesus moves in the opposite direction. We usually expect people to believe first, then behave, and that is followed finally with belonging. We focus a lot of energy on what we believe, what people should believe, and trying to lead them to make a decision to believe. We treat following Jesus like a light switch. It's either on or off. We boil the gospel down to a sales pitch to get people to believe certain things—that they are sinners, that Jesus loves them and died for them, and that if they believe in him, he will give them eternal life.

What if belief works in a different way? Stephanie did not decide one day that she was going to believe in Jesus and follow him. Instead, she discovered that she believed in Jesus, and then she decided to affirm this with others. She was being discipled before she made a formal decision for Christ. In reality, this is how belief in a general sense works in most parts of our lives.[1]

For instance, my father drives Ford trucks. We did not drive Chevys. As a kid, I firmly believed that Fords were far superior to anything Chevrolet could produce. It did not matter what *Motor Trend* said. I believed in Fords because I was surrounded by a way of life that supported that belief.

Most people don't just decide to change what they believe. Beliefs are based on much more than light-switch decisions. Let's imagine that I want to buy a new truck. My natural inclination is to go straight to the Ford dealership and pick one out. However, consider how this might change if over the last six months I rode in a friend's Chevy truck once a week and was surprisingly impressed. Then I started asking him questions about the truck and whether or not he enjoys it. Then I read about what such trucks have to offer, compared features to the competition, and took a close look at any

Chevy truck I saw on the road. After a while, my belief in Ford might waver, and I might even discover that my truck beliefs have shifted. The proclamation of my new beliefs would occur as I drove home in a new Chevy truck.

I've always been impressed by the massive belief expressed on the day of Pentecost after Peter preached a short sermon and called people to repentance. Acts 2 tells us that about three thousand people were baptized as a result. In my imagination, these people were hearing this sermon for the first time and believing, yet this does not make any sense if you actually read the full account. Those people listening already knew a lot about Jesus. They had participated in his crucifixion. Many of them had probably heard Jesus teach. Some would have experienced the miracle of Jesus feeding the five thousand. Others would have witnessed him raising Lazarus from the dead. And even those who did not experience these things firsthand would have likely heard about them through the grapevine. Those who declared their belief in Jesus after Peter's sermon discovered that they believed. Peter helped them to see and understand what they believed about Jesus, and then they professed that through baptism.

Today, we have to create safe places for people to experience Jesus's life through Jesus's followers. As we act in this way, we make room for them to belong with us. This occurs through shared life, over meals, in conversations over fences, or by mutual participation in a local cause. We act by taking the life of the community to them. We open up our life together and include them so that they can see what God is like in our midst.

Stephanie had an opportunity to see God and the gospel as much more than a personal salvation experience. She was able to discover the story of Jesus as the fulfillment of God's promises to redeem the world and to see that she could have a part in God's plan to save the world. She saw the grand story of God and how we as a church were living out that story. She then could start living it and seeing what it looked like from the inside.

# 32

## Gospel Improv

While doing undergraduate studies, I was involved with a student ministry that heavily emphasized sharing the gospel with people who did not know Jesus. We saw hundreds of students embark upon a new relationship with Jesus each year. Every Christmas we took two or three teams to Mexico to do construction work on a church and to share the gospel with anyone who would listen to us. We were taught the importance of being ready to share the gospel at any time with anyone. First Peter 3:15 was woven into my psyche. It reads, "In your hearts revere Christ as Lord. Always be prepared to give an answer to everyone who asks you to give the reason for the hope that you have. But do this with gentleness and respect." I love the way the Message puts it in modern vernacular: "Be ready to speak up and tell anyone who asks why you're living the way you are, and always with the utmost courtesy."

I'm thankful I was taught how to share a solid reason for living the way I do. While riding on a bus once, a friend asked me point-blank, "Why do you believe this stuff?" Within a few minutes, I was able to tell about the "reason for the hope" that I have. Or to put it in the terms of this book, I could explain why I am willing to be a difference maker as opposed to investing my life in other ways of living.

What, then, do we say when it's time to explain the gospel? The word *gospel* means something like "the proclamation of good news." Usually, when we share the gospel, we explain "the plan of salvation," that is, how someone can believe the right things and get saved so that he or she can go to heaven. It focuses on how the death of Jesus applies to our problem of sin and how that can be fixed. While part of the gospel, the plan of salvation falls short of explaining the much larger story of the gospel. The reason for our hope stands on the grand gospel story of the difference-making God. If people want to know this story, we could tell them the story of the entire Bible, but most people won't endure something that long.

Of course, there are many ways to tell the story in brief, but most summaries tend to focus so much on the salvation of the individual that they leave out the bigger picture of what God is doing in our world. People need to hear that God's good news of salvation is about the entire world, not just individuals. I've found that one of the most effective ways to convey this is to use a verse that many have already heard as the basis for telling the gospel story of God. Here's a short way to explain the reason for our hope using John 3:16–17:

> For God so loved the world that he gave his one and only Son, that whoever believes in him shall not perish but have eternal life. For God did not send his Son into the world to condemn the world, but to save the world through him.

God created the world out of love. He created humans to be participants in this love. However, humans chose to reject this love and opt for other ways of life that resulted in death. We see these patterns of death all around us in all kinds of ways. Unlike most people, God did not turn his back on those who rejected him. He did not return rejection for rejection. God continued to love by preparing a way to draw his prized possessions back to himself.

When it became clear that no one could receive and return God's love fully (this is primarily the point of the Old Testament, by the way), God sent his Son Jesus to stand in the place of humans to receive and give love back to the Father. In doing so, he demonstrated what life with God and with others was meant to look like. However, this got Jesus in trouble. People were so accustomed to options other than loving God that they did not approve of the way he was speaking and living, so they killed him on a cross. This death was the death that every human earned for opting out of loving God. Jesus died in our place.

Then Jesus defeated death by rising on the third day. By doing so, he created a pathway for us to enter into his life so that we might love God faithfully. After forty days of walking on the earth, he ascended into heaven and sent the Holy Spirit to live in us and empower us to love God from the inside out.

The Holy Spirit came to work to make the world right and to empower us in the work of making a difference in the midst of those who reject God's love. The Spirit does this through the church, the society of difference makers who participate in God's love and aim to set the world right.

All of us can choose to participate in God's life and love and join him in what he is doing in the world. We do this by repenting, which simply means we turn away from our current ways and ask God to fill us with the life of his Spirit. Then we experience forgiveness, and the power of death is broken in our lives.

That's a very basic summary of the hope within us. Of course, in conversation with people, you would never present it in such a scripted way. That would be awkward to say the least. It works much better when it can be shared conversationally.

Learn to tell it your way, with your words and your improv. Make it your own and let conversations arise as people ask why you make the difference you do.[1]

Can you tell the story of the gospel? Take a few minutes and practice putting this story in your own words. Try doing it aloud. Doing so may feel weird at first, but it's a great way to get this story inside you.

# 33

## Your Improv

The early church called improv the act of witnessing. Acts 1:8 tells us, "But you will receive power when the Holy Spirit comes on you, and you will be my witnesses in Jerusalem, and in all Judea and Samaria, and to the ends of the earth." Actually, the Greek word for witness is the same word from which we get the word *martyr*. To be a witness, as the Bible uses the word, is to demonstrate the message of Christ with the way we live.

Let's think about it this way. What does it mean to be a witness to something? It simply means to offer a testimony. It means that we tell our story, our experience, our perspective, as if we were sitting in a witness box at a court hearing. To share our witness with someone is simply the act of sharing our story of relating to Jesus.

Witnessing contrasts with some of the approaches of talking about Jesus in which we try to convince people that they should be like us and become Jesus followers. When we think it our job to be "convincers," we try to prove that Jesus is worth following. That often means we try to convince others that Jesus is useful, factual, or reasonable.

When we make Jesus into someone who is *useful*, Jesus becomes a commodity to bait people into Christianity. So we try to convince people that they will have a better life—that they will be happier and have more money and fewer struggles—if they follow Jesus. Even though Jesus does transform our lives for the better, we usually bait people with a version of Jesus that can help them attain the American dream. We use Jesus as a commodity and settle for false advertising.

If we feel it necessary to make Jesus *factual*, we try to convince others about the "right way" of thinking about the historicity of Jesus. Many people shy away from talking about Jesus because they feel they don't have enough information to address questions people might have. So they opt out and leave witnessing to the "professionals" who are trained in all of the historical stuff. While there is a place for historical support for faith, people need much more than facts in order to enter into Christ's life.

Whenever we feel that witnessing is about proving Jesus to be *reasonable*—that Jesus makes more sense than any other option—we focus on the logic of following Jesus. Even though there is logical evidence that proves that following Jesus is the most reasonable choice, debates about apologetics rarely convince people to change their minds. My friend Greg Boyd collected a series of letters that he shared with his atheistic father over a period of three years in a book called *Letters from a Skeptic*. In the end, his father gave his life to Jesus. When reading these letters, you might assume that Greg's theological arguments finally won his father over. While this is partially true, Greg also shares how the root issue was not about apologetics or the reasonableness of faith. The root issue was related to his dad's anger at God over the death of Greg's mom. Reasonableness alone did not lead him down the path to God.[1]

Being a witness is far more than arguing for usefulness, facts, or reasonableness. People need witnesses who are willing to simply tell their stories about their relationship with Jesus. People can argue over the value of Jesus in modern life. They can challenge historical facts. They can present alternative reasons that make other approaches sound more reasonable. But the one thing you have to share is your story, your improv, and how Jesus is shaping you to fit into his story.

The challenge for us is to learn to tell our stories well, to share our stories improvisationally in a way that is a healthy response to a need. Most people tell it too quickly—"Yes, I'm a Christian. Jesus means everything."—because they just don't know what to say. Others say far too much. They provide such a long version that no one wants to hear it.

If you want to witness well, learn to tell your story in two to four minutes. Use this short outline to help you write out your story.

Your life before knowing Christ

_____

_____

_____

How you encountered Christ for the first time

_____

_____

_____

How Christ has changed your life

_____

_____

_____

# 34

## Joining the Improv Cast

During a rehearsal for our high school performance of *Romeo and Juliet*, I was standing backstage with some friends. I played Mercutio, the crazy friend of Romeo who was killed in a sword fight. My character had already died off at this point of the rehearsal, and I had time to waste. One of the stagehands, Jack, shared how he was going through a tough time. He was a bit of a loner and was prone to depression. That night, it all came to a head and he was willing to open up.

I began to share about Jesus and how he could bring peace into Jack's life. I explained how Jesus came and died for our sins so that we could be free from a life of alienation from God. He was all ears. I asked him if he wanted to pray to have a relationship with God, and to my shock he said he did. So I invited him to pray the sinner's prayer. I prayed, and then he repeated after me. It went something like this:

> Thank you, God, for loving me. I know I am a sinner in need of your grace. Thank you for sending your Son to die in my place for my sins. Come into my life and be my Savior and Lord. Amen.

I walked across the room and gave him an awkward hug, and then we returned to the rehearsal.

A couple weeks later, I was giving him a ride. As I drove, I explained to him that the next step was to get involved with a church. The conversation was even more awkward than the hug because I did not have any good reasons for attending church. I had great reasons to invite him into a personal relationship with God, but the invitation to join church life did not make as much sense. Going to church was just something good Christians were supposed to do.

In retrospect, I was telling him that church was similar to becoming a spectator at a play. Now that he had a personal relationship with Jesus, he had his ticket to observe what God was doing through other people who could minister to him.

To my knowledge, he never got baptized and never participated in a church. I did not do a very good job of convincing him that he needed to become a spiritual spectator. And quite honestly, I don't blame him.

Now I wonder if things would have been different if I had invited Jack to become part of the improv cast of being a Jesus follower. What if I had not told him to join the church so that it might prove useful to his personal spiritual life and make him a better Christian? What if I had raised the bar—a lot—and told him that having a personal relationship with Jesus meant that we were joining in the Jesus way of life, a movement of difference makers?

Many people may feel a personal need for a personal Savior. After their personal needs are met, their need for a personal Savior wanes. When that happens, their need for Jesus and Jesus stuff, like the church, also wanes. When we tack church on top of personal salvation, church becomes a spectator club we participate in when it proves useful to us, or it becomes an ideology club that feeds our need to prove we are more right than anybody else.

Eric Lerew is a creative church leader in Chicago who has an incredible ability to talk about Jesus to those who don't know him. Recently, he told me about a conversation with a woman who told him that her life was working quite well, and she felt no need for the change that Jesus might bring. The normal way I've been taught to proceed is to tell her that she is a sinner like everyone else and that she needs to see that reality and repent of the pride that keeps her from seeing her sin. Eric took a different approach. He asked her, "Are you satisfied with the state of the world? For instance, are you satisfied that sex trafficking is such a big part of the world, even right here in Chicago?" Of course she responded, "No! Of course not." Then he asked, "How is your life contributing to the betterment of the world?" This led to what it means to be a Jesus follower. He turned the conversation away from her own personal well-being to help her see what God is doing in the world and how she might join in. He wanted to help her see that being a Jesus follower is about being a member of a difference-making society that is participating in God's redemption of everything.

The invitation to follow Jesus is not simply a personal invitation to go to heaven one day. When we limit the invitation to personal salvation, we lead people to think that salvation is all about them, and they may very well miss the reality of God's love. However, when we invite them to follow Jesus as a member of a difference-making improv cast, they get the experience of personal salvation as part of the package.

# 35

## Restorative Improv

I don't remember much from my high school physics class, except that there was lots of math involved. One thing stuck, though: the second law of thermodynamics. In its most basic form, it states that everything tends toward entropy. In popular language, everything tends toward chaos unless work from the outside is put into managing it. Anything left to itself will gradually move toward disorder. This is illustrated in the movie *I Am Legend*, in which we observe New York City after almost the entire population has been wiped out by a virus. No one was there to bring creative order to the city, and as a result, grass grew through the streets, buildings were collapsing, and all the systems developed to sustain life fell apart.

I see this reality in my closet, when I walk into my office, or while spending time with our children. Disorder happens even when no one does anything. Order, I have found, actually requires a great deal of concentrated creativity. We see this illustrated in the opening words of the Bible in the creation story. The heavens and the earth were a waste and a void.

Chaos reigned. Darkness ruled. The Spirit moved across the waters, and the creative order of God rolled out. The Spirit of God is present through history in the ongoing work of creation, sustaining and growing what God began. Without this continuing work of creation, chaos would take over.

Take a few minutes to think about your neighborhood using the neighborhood exegesis questions in chapter 16. Where are the places of chaos that need the redemptive action of the Spirit?

Most often the chaos comes in the form of an -ism: individualism, sexism, racism, isolationism, consumerism, workaholism, and other -isms that shape our lives in ways we don't even recognize. Jesus came to set us free from the -isms of our culture. We most often overlook such life patterns because we assume that public issues such as these belong beyond the bounds of the church. When we see only how the gospel applies to our private lives, it is difficult to imagine how it can apply to matters such as how we abuse the environment, how people of color are neglected by governmental systems, how people are trained in the workplace to worship money, or how immigrants have trouble integrating into the local culture. We fail to see how the hidden idols of culture, such as possessions, power, and prestige, are crushing our souls.

Joining the Spirit in making a creative difference involves the creativity of bringing order to chaos. If you have ever been a part of a creative project, you know that there is an unknown element to creativity. It requires ingenuity, time, and unpredictable steps. Creative improv confronts the -isms that subtly destroy life around us and raise up an alternative way of living.

Most of this improv comes in small ways. Weeding a garden may not seem like a significant act when growing vegetables, but skip a couple weeks and see what happens. In the same way, having regular conversations with neighbors who are driven by fear and caught in a never-ending cycle of workaholism may not seem like it has a huge kingdom impact, but without those conversations, how will they see Jesus in you? How will you learn their needs and respond with service? How will you know how to pray for them?

Then again, you may come to realize that there are more obvious -isms at work in your neighborhood. Maybe there's an apartment complex primarily occupied by undocumented families who cannot afford to feed their families and cannot get the help they need because they are afraid of deportation. What if you work with two or three families and take a grill and a bunch of hot dogs over on Tuesday nights to feed the kids and play with them? Then you get to listen to their stories, see their pain, and find out more ways to creatively address the chaos.

Maybe you discover that the isolation of your neighborhood is a controlling force. With a few friends, you could begin to host a monthly gathering at a local park for your neighbors. Get involved with the local neighborhood association. Conversations will arise. People will connect. People will see the life of Jesus demonstrated through you.

Maybe you discover that you have two neighbors who are recently widowed. Then, through conversations, you realize that there are many elderly people who live nearby who need to experience creative improv.

Maybe you learn that there is a battered women's home near your church building.

Maybe you learn of an old friend who is the victim of domestic violence.

Chaos is everywhere. Creative redemption is roaming over the face of chaos. We make a difference when we get specific and care enough to get involved.

# Engaging Your World by Being a Faithful Presence

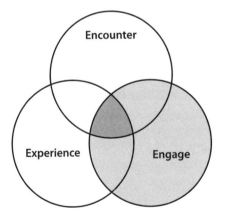

## *Lectio Divina* for Part 6

*All this I have spoken while still with you. But the Advocate, the Holy Spirit, whom the Father will send in my name, will teach you all things and will remind you of everything I have said to you. Peace I leave with you; my peace I give you. I do not give to you as the world gives. Do not let your hearts be troubled and do not be afraid.* (John 14:25–27)

**Read**

**Reflect**

**Respond**

**Remain**

# 36

## Shalom Creation Shops

One night, I was browsing the book aisles at Target. I found the typical bestsellers, thrillers, vampire books, and adventure stories for teenagers. But one topic stood out. I found three bestselling titles about Christians having an afterlife experience before their bodies were resuscitated. We shouldn't be shocked about the fascination with the afterlife. The question of whether or not you get to go to heaven has been the focus of much preaching, and many people think that following Jesus is all about punching their ticket to heaven.

However, the words of Jesus call us into much more than that. Mark summarizes the beginning of Jesus's public ministry with these words: "Jesus went into Galilee, proclaiming the good news of God. 'The time has come,' he said. 'The kingdom of God has come near. Repent and believe the good news!'" (Mark 1:14–15). The word for good news here is the same as the word for gospel.

The good news of the kingdom of God is revealed in the presence and ministry of Jesus Christ. The listeners that day no longer needed to await the coming of the Messiah. Jesus came to offer good news, and it would result in concrete, tangible, visible manifestations. The kingdom of God had then and has now a concrete, "right now" meaning. It is not something that comes after death, some kind of spiritual, nonphysical reality that has nothing to do with the everyday realities we face.

Someday, Jesus will return to restore justice and redeem all of creation. There is a heaven, and there will continue to be debates about who gets in and who does not. But the Bible never turns the kingdom of God into a private, disembodied experience that has nothing to do with life on earth. Jesus wants to reveal the beauty of his kingdom in the midst of the evil, abuse, and ugliness in our world. He wants to provide an experience of the good news in very concrete ways.

This is why Jesus said to his disciples, "'Peace be with you! As the Father has sent me, I am sending you.' And with that he breathed on them and said, 'Receive the Holy Spirit'" (John 20:21–22). Jesus fulfilled the promise he made to the disciples after washing their feet when he said, "All this I have spoken while still with you. But the Advocate, the Holy Spirit, whom the Father will send in my name, will teach you all things and will remind you of everything I have said to you. Peace I leave with you; my peace I give you. I do not give to you as the world gives. Do not let your hearts be troubled and do not be afraid" (John 14:25–27).

The Holy Spirit remains as God's faithful presence, continuing the good news of the kingdom of God.[1] The Spirit reveals the concrete presence of God in our midst. God remains with us in the here and now, changing, moving, restoring. The calling of God is on our lives not so we can wait for an escape from the problems of this world as we live in fear. God reveals his faithful presence to us through the Spirit so that we might reveal his faithfulness in the world.

The Spirit comes to set up a shalom creation shop in the midst of us. *Shalom* is the Hebrew word we translate as "peace," but it means much more than what we mean by that one word. It goes far beyond a lack of conflict to mean things such as wholeness, completeness, restfulness, unity, and life as it was designed to be. Shalom cannot be dictated, legislated, or programmed. It cannot be forced, taught, or inspired by those over us or outside of us. It can only be embraced, lived, and fought for.

The Spirit is creating this through God's people in specific locations in the midst of life. A particular church inhabits a particular place in the midst of a larger place. A particular small group lives out the life of Christ on a particular street or in a particular neighborhood. As a community of God's people lives faithfully together, the Spirit generates shalom.

What's required of us to bear this faithful presence of shalom? We remain. We stay put. We put down roots. We don't bounce around doing a little ministry here and a little ministry there. We don't determine whether or not we stay based on how people respond to Christ and change their lives. I know missionaries who work with people in Southeast Asia where thousands upon thousands of churches are being birthed. I also know missionaries who work in Western Europe where it takes years to see people embrace a relationship with Jesus. The call is to faithful presence, not to quick success.

Staying put in a particular location goes against the flow of our culture. People move and are uprooted in modern society more than ever in history. My friend Tyler and his wife have set up shop on the east side of St. Paul. They have worked hard to read their neighborhood by getting to know the people on their street. Tyler likes working on cars, so he does so with his garage open so that people can see what he does, and he uses this skill to serve others. For years, he has led a block party that gathers the people around a common calling. And in the midst of an area of town that is known for violence, theft, and isolation, Tyler and his wife have worked for the common good of all. They have done this by remaining, by staying put.

Making a difference sometimes happens quickly, but most things that have a lasting impact take time. I have a friend who has been praying for her husband to join in God's difference-making life for nine years. Recently, he told her, "Through all of the ups and downs, you have remained true." He's not there yet, but he sees the little stuff, and it's the little stuff that matters. The Great Wall of China was built one brick at a time. With every little thing you do that lines up with the kingdom, you add another brick that makes a difference. Maybe it's remaining faithful to an unbelieving spouse without trying to nag him or her into salvation. Maybe it's tutoring a kid even when he shows no interest. Maybe it's sitting with a widow who has little to say. One day we may be surprised by the difference we made.

# 37

## Practicing the Presence of Church

Sometimes it can feel like church is just an add-on that simply helps us do life, an optional thing that varies in importance depending on how we feel from week to week. Its importance wanes for many when they are struggling in relationships with others in the church or in a small group. It's tempting to think that the grass is greener at the church down the road. So why go to church? Eugene Peterson responds to this question: "The short answer is because the Holy Spirit formed it to be a colony of heaven in the country of death. . . . Church is the core element in the strategy of the Holy Spirit for providing human witness and physical presence to the Jesus-inaugurated kingdom of God in this world. It is not that kingdom complete, but it is a witness to that kingdom."[1]

No church is perfect, but that's not the point. We often miss out on what God is doing through the church because we expect it to be exciting and stimulating. We expect it to meet our needs, and then we go about our normal lives. Of course, that is the pattern of our culture. We participate in very little that fails to meet our needs or entertain us. It is impossible not to carry this mentality into the church. We consume church.

Unless we confront this life of consumption, we will never grow up to practice a life that makes a difference. We will bounce around from place to place and fail to stay put long enough with a specific group of people in a specific place to be a specific colony of heaven. Making a difference requires a mentality of investment, not one of consumption. As long as we consume church—in whatever our preferred form—we will miss out on the experience of being God's colony in a country of death. Being a part of the church requires us to stay put, to contribute, to work through difficulties, and to love others even when it would be easier to leave.

Instead of running every time we get offended or we don't like something, we need to remain, to develop a life pattern of being present in relationships, and to allow God to work through us over time. Most of the time, it's the people with whom we are relating—through the normal ups and downs—whom God uses to help us grow. We learn to practice being a heavenly colony together, and thereby we make a difference. And when we do this in a way that allows others to observe our faithful presence with one another, church becomes much more than an interesting option for Sunday mornings.

Imagine a church in first-century Ephesus. People didn't meet in a designated building where outsiders couldn't see what was going on. Christians met in homes that were adjacent to other homes and streets less than six feet wide. Cities like Ephesus were small and crowded. There was not a line between private and public life like we have today. Everybody knew what was going on. When Paul and his team entered Ephesus and people became Jesus followers, or when someone was healed or when the church was worshiping, many people would have talked about it. Things that we relegate to the inner or private life of the church—like worship, preaching, and prayer services—would have been visible for all to see.

This is why we must think of the church as living out the life of Jesus locally. We must think of ways to live the life of worship so that people can observe the life of Christ in us. Today, this often happens as small communities share life within specific neighborhoods and work for the common good of that specific location. They use homes, coffee shops, parks, restaurants, and other public places to gather. They remain over time in these places so that others see who they are, how they live, and how God works through them. By doing so, they become priests of light in the midst of darkness.

For a church to be a faithful presence in a neighborhood, the church must actually experience the faithful presence of God. If there is anything that should be the hallmark of God's people, it is God's presence. With one quick reading of the book of Acts, it becomes immediately clear that the people of God had an unseen partner who was really the primary partner. It could even be argued that without God's presence there is no church.

Once I invited a friend named Armando to church. He did not know Jesus personally, but we had talked about faith and I'd shared my testimony with him. He said he was ready to check out a church service. After the meeting, we sat talking in my car. He was in tears. All he could say was, "I felt God's presence. God was so real in the worship." It was not hard to introduce him to Jesus at that point. I led him in a short prayer.

Worship is a mark of God's people. And when we worship, God's presence is made real. Worship shifts our focus from ourselves and our circumstances and helps us to see God for who he really is. Without worship, it's too easy to make God into a vending machine who offers self-help products to meet our needs.

If we don't have the presence of God, what do we have to offer the world? We are called a "royal priesthood" (1 Pet. 2:9), which means we have one hand connected to God's presence and one hand connected to those who need God.

We are God's "matchmakers" in a way, offering people a new reality that comes as we connect their hands to the hand of God. Worship connects us to God and empowers us to offer something real and tangible as we connect with those in our world.

# 38

## Presence Takes Practice

No one gets good at something without practice. I've been a fan of the Texas Rangers since 1978. Back then, I'd listen to the games on my little transistor radio, hardly ever missing one. During their run to the World Series in 2011, I had the joy of watching Nelson Cruz tie the record for the most home runs hit in the play-offs. However, a few years before, no one thought such a thing possible. In the minor leagues, Cruz would dominate, but major-league pitchers would exploit a weakness in his swing, and he struck out far too often to stay on a major-league team.

Then one coach saw potential. He taught Cruz to swing the bat in a way that eliminated the weakness. Fixing his swing required him to retrain his muscles. He had to work to create new muscle memory so that the new way of swinging became a habit. This required daily effort, focused attention, and months and months of repetition. This was not a quick fix.

Most of the time, we like quick fixes and easy answers to difficult questions. We want a magical plan that will change everything. But there are no quick fixes to becoming a difference maker. Doing so requires more than simply reading this book and listening to a few sermons. That's the start. Information is helpful—just as Nelson Cruz needed a coach to give him a new way to hit—but real change comes through repetition and practice.

The Spirit of God forms us through practice to live his way as a people. Jesus prayed, "Your kingdom come, your will be done, on earth as it is in heaven" (Matt. 6:10). How does this occur? God's kingdom comes as the people of God do the things we have been talking about in this book over and over. The kingdom of God is not a one-hit wonder. As we make choices about difference-making practices, our habits change. And as our habits change, we develop a difference-making character.

Difference-making choices lead to difference-making actions.

Difference-making actions lead to difference-making practices.

Difference-making practices lead to difference-making habits.

Difference-making habits lead to difference-making character.

Difference-making character creates faithful presence.

We cannot jump into making a huge difference. We need to start by practicing smaller differences, some of which will be awkward at first.

When our second son, Gavin, played T-ball, the coach would lead the team in thirty minutes of practice before the games. On one night, Gavin traipsed beneath a light rain and tried in vain to climb some playground bars as he waited for the game to start. Then he came back to the car. I told him he needed to throw the ball with his team. He said to me, "It's just practice. I don't need to. I'm already good."

The apostle Paul uses the imagery of training for athletic competition to talk about his preparation:

> Not that I have already obtained all this, or have already arrived at my goal, but I press on to take hold of that for which Christ Jesus took hold of me. Brothers and sisters, I do not consider myself yet to have taken hold of it. But one thing I do: Forgetting what is behind and straining toward what is ahead, I press on toward the goal to win the prize for which God has called me heavenward in Christ Jesus. (Phil. 3:12–14)

In sports, the games are won or lost on the practice field long before the official competitions begin. The same is true for difference makers. Conferences, seminars, classes, and written resources may get us started, but the real training comes when we practice. We actually require a lot less information than we are led to believe. For instance, if you walk into a bookstore, you will find hundreds of plans for getting your body in shape and losing weight, but the biggest part of the training is just doing it.

If we want to make a difference in our world, then we need to practice. Knowing the right information won't help us if we don't act on it. We practice by worshiping. We practice by sharing meals together and receiving communion and living in community. We practice by sacrificing for each other. We practice by praying, by fasting, by waiting on God's presence, by reading the Scriptures. We practice through obedience, submission, and generosity. We offer hospitality to those who cannot offer it in return.

We practice faithful presence in the midst of everyday life long before anyone expresses a willingness to receive it. We don't know when the right opportunity will come up, but because we have been present, people are much more likely to turn to us. Then, when a need, a crisis, or a problem arises, our practice will have prepared us for the right action.

Most of the time the best practice happens when no one is looking. When I have a private encounter with God, my love for others increases. Often I don't even see it because the encounter with God shapes me from the inside out. When I'm not encountering God, I find I have little energy for conversations with my neighbors. When I am encountering God, I find that conversations happen without my even trying. This is why difference making is about encountering God, experiencing one another, and engaging our world. We make a difference out of the $E^3$ center.

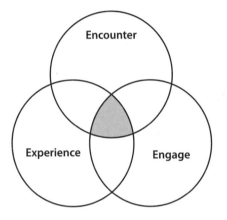

What we practice in private shapes our public encounters with others, and our public engagement with our neighbors and networks shapes our private practice. The best way to learn and grow in our practice is through the ups and downs of trial and error. Failure should drive us to our knees and lead us to deeper conversations with others on the same journey. The only way to become a difference maker is to keep at it.

# 39

## Practicing Three Things

Formerly, the Western church thought about church as something we did in the home country and missions as something that was done overseas. Pastors led local churches, and missionaries traveled to far lands to tell "pagans" about Jesus. But this is no longer the case. We don't need to go overseas to talk with people who either know very little about Jesus or have rejected what they do know. In more cases than we want to admit, these people don't think the modern church has answers to the questions of life or solutions to the crises they face.

Faithful presence calls us to live as local missionaries even though we have jobs that pay the bills. Whether or not you are a missionary isn't a choice. What kind of missionary will you be? What will you do to live out a faithful presence in the midst of your neighborhood?

Of course, the answer to these questions lies at the heart of this book. The process of paying attention, reflecting, acting, and remaining as a faithful presence will take us deeper and deeper into the life of our neighborhoods and open doors for us to carry the life of God into dark places. These actions are like four horizontal threads that run parallel to one another. As we sew them, our lives are woven into our neighborhoods.

Woven into these four horizontal threads are three vertical threads that represent three practices that shape how we pay attention, reflect, act, and remain as a faithful presence. There are many ways to engage our neighborhoods, but almost all of them can be traced back to one of these three core practices:[1]

- Hospitality: welcoming the stranger, the disenfranchised, the dislocated, the one without community. You need not go any farther than next-door neighbors in most cases.

- Generosity: offering life, resources, and blessing to those who think they must earn everything in life.

- Forgiveness: offering freedom in a world where people are treated with violence, control, and manipulation.

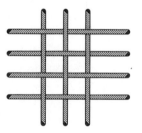

This is love in action, the practices that should be the primary marks of the church. The apostle Paul put it this way:

Share with the Lord's people who are in need. Practice hospitality. Bless those who persecute you; bless and do not curse. Rejoice with those who rejoice; mourn with those who mourn. Live in harmony with one another. Do not be proud, but be willing to associate with people of low position. Do not be conceited. Do not repay anyone evil for evil. Be careful to do what is right in the eyes of everyone. If it is possible, as far as it depends on you, live at peace with everyone. (Rom. 12:13–18)

As we weave these three practices into our daily lives, we offer our neighborhoods an alternative way of life, a hopeful option to the dominant patterns that steal true life. For instance, the Old Testament stories speak to how the Israelites were always trying to copy the patterns of the reputable nations of their times. They wanted the privilege, the possessions, and the power that they observed in Egypt, Assyria, and Babylon. This is most clear in the story of King Solomon when he sought after these three things instead of the things of God.

Sadly, the idols of privilege, possessions, and power continue to shape today's neighborhoods. When we idolize privilege, we cut off the weak, the widows, the orphans, and the sick. When we idolize possessions, we horde, we work too much, and we live in fear of losing it all. When we idolize power, we run over others, we fight for ourselves, and we treat one another with violence and manipulation. Basically, it's the old story of those on top fighting to stay there and those beneath trying to work their way up. Jesus came denouncing these ways, embodying an alternative. Jesus came as the footwashing God, inviting others to join him. Instead of seeking after privilege, he came as a hospitable servant. Instead of fighting for possessions, he generously shared life. Instead of the violence of power, he offered the grace of forgiveness. Difference makers follow suit, embodying God's faithful presence in their neighborhoods through these three practices.

Now, before you make this harder than it needs to be, consider this. What if you do something as simple as having a neighbor over for a meal once per month? Then you do this every month for the next few years. What kind of impact might this have on your neighborhood? What kind of conversations might happen? How might your community become safer? What resources might be shared? How might life become more enjoyable? This is how God's hope for this world multiplies into visible reality.

## Part 6 Activity

### Host a Meal

Many in our culture are out of practice when it comes to hosting a meal. Here are a few things to consider as you do this activity:

- Invite a neighbor for a meal. Tell them there is no occasion or reason and you are not trying to sell them something. You just want to get to know them better. Ask them to bring a simple item to contribute to the meal. People feel better if they can contribute something.
- Cook a simple meal. Don't make the evening elaborate or complicated. This can be intimidating to guests.
- Try to have most of the meal already cooked when the guests arrive so that you don't have to focus on the tasks and can pay attention to the guests. Maybe have finger foods available for snacking. This creates a comfortable environment for sharing.
- Ask questions. Show interest in your guests. Find out about their jobs, their interests, their family, etc. People like to talk about themselves, so give them the chance. And of course, as you are conversing, you will have opportunities to share about your own life.

# 40

## Presence for the Sake of the World

Recently, I was talking with some friends about how we make a difference in others' lives. People shared stories about friends, adult children, spouses, relatives, neighbors, and co-workers who do not know God's love. People shared their great passion for these people. Along with the passion, they expressed anxiety about the fact that the world around them is not changing as they think it should. We talked about our pain regarding why people don't follow Jesus and what it really takes to make a difference.

I used to lead training sessions about ministering to people who are not followers of Christ. As an opening exercise, I would ask the seminar participants to respond to a few questions.

Question: Who influenced you the most to become a Jesus follower?

Answer: Ninety percent of the room would say it was a friend, co-worker, family member, or neighbor.

Question: What did that person do to influence you?

Answer: Almost always the answer was something like, "They listened to me. They cared. And they told me the truth as a friend."

Question: How many people influenced you?

Answer: Rarely would anyone respond with something other than "many."

Question: How long did it take for you to come to the point where you were willing to become a committed Jesus follower?

Answer: Most often the answer was, "An extended period of time." Some would say, "Years."

The answers to these questions reveal the importance of faithful presence. Often we equate difference making with confrontational talks with strangers, done alone in such a way that produces immediate results. This is the opposite of reality in most cases. Whether we are hoping for someone to begin a new walk with Christ, standing with a family stuck in generational poverty, or investing in the betterment of a local neighborhood, faithful presence makes all the difference. Loving our family members through the ups and downs makes a difference. Fighting for what's right in our neighborhoods and cities makes a difference. Investing in local businesses that can hire local employees makes a difference. Cleaning up a local street over a period of months and even years makes a difference.

As we are present as God's people in our neighborhoods and with our networks, some of us will plow the ground, some will plant the seeds, some will water, and others will harvest (see 1 Cor. 3:6–9). Love isn't quick and easy.

In a conversation with some friends, Barry shared, "Following Jesus is not about trying to create Jesus in every situation but in every situation letting Jesus be creative in and through you." With that one statement, he captured the heart of difference makers. We are not called to make things happen for God so that the world will change. We are invited to join the Father, Son, and Spirit in the life God is creating in all of the world.

God the Father sent the Son for the sake of the world. The same is true of the Spirit, and we participate in what the Spirit is doing for the sake of the world. God has a dream of redeeming all of creation, and we fall short of manifesting God's love unless we are seeking to carry this redemption into every dimension of life.[1]

Faithful presence for the sake of the world. Presence for the sake of our neighborhoods. For our streets. For our workplaces. As we make choices to encounter the God of love, to experience love with others and engage our world, the Holy Spirit forms us to possess the character of difference makers. You have embarked upon a journey of learning to live from the $E^3$ center. Already the Spirit of God has changed you to reflect more of the character of a difference maker. You are taking on the virtues that naturally impact our neighbors, our neighborhoods, our cities, our countries, and our world.

As you conclude this book, take a few minutes to reflect on how you have been changed in these four areas:

1. Paying attention to what is going on in your neighborhood and networks
2. Reflecting through prayer to see what God is saying
3. Acting to meet needs you see
4. Being a faithful presence by staying put

Closing Prayer:

*Lord, make me an instrument of your peace.*
    Where there is hatred, let me sow love.
    Where there is injury, pardon.
    Where there is doubt, faith.
    Where there is despair, hope.
    Where there is darkness, light.

Where there is sadness, joy.
O Divine Master,
grant that I may not so much seek to be consoled, as
 to console;
to be understood, as to understand;
to be loved, as to love.
For it is in giving that we receive.
It is in pardoning that we are pardoned,
and it is in dying that we are born to Eternal Life.
Amen.

attributed to St. Francis of Assisi

# Appendix

# Discussion Guide for Small Groups

**Part 1**

*Icebreaker*

• Who is someone you would describe as a difference maker?

*Focus Scripture: John 13:3–5*

• What stands out to you from this passage of Scripture?
• When you hear "putting love where love is not," what comes to mind?
• Why is it important to see that it's God's mission and not ours?
• What do you think God is already doing in your neighborhood? If you have never thought of God at work in this way, what might it look like for this to occur?
• What do you think God wants to do in your neighborhood?

## Part 2

### Icebreaker

- Who was your favorite teacher in school? What did they do that impacted you?

### Focus Scripture: John 13:34–35

- As you think about this Scripture reading, what stands out?
- How might the love that Jesus's disciples had for one another be a witness to others? How might the love we have for one another in the church make a difference today in the world around us?
- Read Luke 10:1–12. Why do you think Jesus sent people out in teams?
- What are some of the things that stand in the way of our ability to work in a difference-making team?
- Think about your time. Maybe you cannot simply add an activity on top of all the things you are doing. Is there something in your life you could sacrifice to make room for making a difference?
- What unique strengths can you contribute to a team?

## Part 3

### Icebreaker

- What easily distracts you and causes you to lose focus?

### Focus Scripture: John 13:12–17

- As you hear the words of Jesus in this passage, what impresses you? What does it mean to be a difference-making foot washer?
- When someone listens to you—really listens—how does that make you feel? How do you think it makes others feel when you don't really listen to them?

- How is paying attention to people an expression of God's love?

- What are some things that stand in the way of your paying attention to your neighbors and those in your networks?

- How can God speak to you about needs as you pay attention to others? To your neighbors? To your neighborhoods?

- What are some specific ways that you can pay attention to others in your ordinary life (work, home, school, restaurants)?

## Part 4

### Icebreaker

- How have the prayers of someone else changed you?

### Focus Scripture: John 15:4–5

- What from this passage stands out to you?

- Why is listening to how God wants you to make a difference so important?

- What can happen when we assume we know how to minister to others and we don't take the time to listen?

- Your ordinary, daily connecting with God in prayer can change the world. What's your reaction to that statement? How might your prayers change if you really believed this?

- How can the group pray together in a way that makes a difference in our neighborhoods?

Suggestion: Ask everyone in the group to contribute two names from their tic-tac-toe activity. Spend time praying for those on this list and continue to do so throughout the rest of this study.

## Part 5

### Icebreaker

- Share a time when you helped another person and really enjoyed it.

### Focus Scripture: John 15:13–16

- What does this passage mean to you?
- Why is the way we act or respond to specific needs in our world similar to improvisational acting?
- Why is your testimony about your life with Jesus so important?
- How can conversations with friends lead to natural opportunities to have a conversation about Jesus?
- Read 1 Peter 3:15. What is the hope you have? Are people seeing this hope in your life?

## Part 6

### Icebreaker

- What has changed in your life through this series?

### Focus Scripture: John 20:25–27

- What impressions do you have about this passage of Scripture?
- How is the offer of "peace" or wholeness connected to remaining or staying put in a specific place?
- Why is staying put and ministering to people over an extended time important?
- What are some practical ways to make a difference over the long term?

- Why is hospitality so crucial to being a faithful presence? What impact might having a neighbor over for a meal once per month have on your neighborhood?
- Why are worship and church so important to making a difference?

# Notes

### Introduction

1. David Benner, *Opening to God* (Downers Grove, IL: InterVarsity, 2010), 51–52.
2. Ibid., 52.
3. Ibid., 52.
4. Ibid., 52.

### Chapter 2: Participating in God's Difference

1. This story is told by Mark Lau Branson and Juan F. Martinez in their book *Churches, Cultures and Leadership* (Downers Grove, IL: InterVarsity, 2011), 73–74.

### Chapter 3: Dancing with God

1. For an excellent introduction to how the Trinity relates to the way God's people make a difference in the world, see Craig Van Gelder and Dwight Zscheile, *The Missional Church in Perspective* (Grand Rapids: Baker Academic, 2011).
2. The questions What is God already doing in the world? and What does God want to do? were first posed in this fashion by Craig Van Gelder in his book *The Ministry of the Missional Church* (Grand Rapids: Baker, 2007), 59–61.

### Chapter 4: Inside Out Difference Makers

1. Christopher L. Heuertz and Christine D. Pohl, *Friendship at the Margins: Discovering Mutuality in Service and Mission* (Downers Grove, IL: InterVarsity, 2010), 31.
2. Ibid., 33.
3. Lesslie Newbigin put it this way: "All of us except those at the very bottom have a vested interest in keeping [natural chains of authority in place], for as long

as we duly submit to those above us we are free to bear down on those below us. The action of Jesus subverts this order and threatens to destabilize all society. Peter's protest is the protest of normal human nature" (*The Light Has Come* [Grand Rapids: Eerdmans, 1982], 168).

### Chapter 5: What Kind of God?

1. This activity is based on the book *America's Four Gods* by Paul Froese and Christopher Bader (New York: Oxford University Press, 2010). I adapted this exercise from an activity led by my friend Kevin Callagan, one of the pastors at Woodland Hills Church.

### Chapter 6: What Is God Already Doing?

1. This definition of agape love comes from Paul Eddy, a systematic theologian who teaches at Bethel University.
2. See C. S. Lewis, *The Four Loves* (New York: Harcourt Books, 1920).

### Chapter 8: Me? A Difference Maker?

1. Rodney Stark, *The Rise of Christianity* (New York: HarperCollins, 1996), 73–94.

### Chapter 9: Your Unique Difference

1. For a look at Luke 10 as it applies to engaging people in our neighborhoods, see Alan Roxburgh, *Missional: Joining God in the Neighborhood* (Grand Rapids: Baker, 2011).
2. See Marcus Buckingham and Donald O. Clifton, *Now, Discover Your Strengths* (New York: Free Press, 2001).

### Chapter 14: The Reality of Teamwork

1. Mike Tatlock, *Faith in Real Life* (Grand Rapids: Zondervan, 2010), 195.
2. A couple of helpful books on this topic include Stephen Arterburn and Jack Felton, *Toxic Faith* (Colorado Springs: Waterbrook Press, 2001); and David Johnson and Jeff VanVonderan, *Subtle Power of Spiritual Abuse* (Minneapolis: Bethany, 2005).

### Chapter 16: Paying Attention

1. Simon Carey Holt, *God Next Door* (Victoria, Australia: Acorn Press, 2007), 103.
2. Adapted from ibid., 104.

### Chapter 17: Neighbors and Networks

1. I adapted this idea from Jay Pathak of the Mile High Vineyard in Arvada, Colorado, as reported in Matt Branaugh, "Know Your Neighbors," *Leadership Journal* (Winter 2012): 45–48.

## Chapter 18: Going Local

1. Wendell Berry, *The Art of the Commonplace* (Berkeley, CA: Centerpoint, 2002), 11.
2. Dietrich Bonhoeffer, *Life Together*, trans. Daniel Boesch (Minneapolis: Fortress, 1996), 27.

## Chapter 23: Listen Up

1. Henri Nouwen, *The Only Necessary Thing* (New York: Crossroad Publishing, 1999), 36.
2. N. T. Wright, *Scripture and the Authority of God* (New York: HarperOne, 2011), 31–32.

## Chapter 25: Praying in the Moments

1. This is what Richard Foster calls it in his book *Prayer: Finding the Heart's True Home* (New York: HarperOne, 1992).
2. N. T. Wright, *Bringing the Church to the World* (Minneapolis: Bethany, 1992), 211.

## Chapter 29: The Action of Improv

1. This idea of improv in the church came from the excellent book by Samuel Wells titled *Improvisation* (Grand Rapids: Brazos, 2004).
2. Dallas Willard, *Hearing God* (Downers Grove, IL: InterVarsity, 1999), 95.

## Chapter 31: Inclusive Improv

1. This thought was derived from Rick Richardson, *Evangelism Outside the Box* (Downers Grove, IL: InterVarsity, 2000).

## Chapter 32: Gospel Improv

1. If you have a desire to pursue ways to talk about the gospel of Jesus further, I recommend two books: Scot McKnight, *The King Jesus Gospel* (Grand Rapids: Zondervan, 2011); and N. T. Wright, *Simply Jesus* (New York: HarperOne, 2012).

## Chapter 33: Your Improv

1. If you have a friend who is dealing with issues regarding the reasonableness of following Jesus, it's hard to beat Gregory A. Boyd and Edward K. Boyd, *Letters from a Skeptic: A Son Wrestles with His Father's Questions about Christianity* (Colorado Springs: David C. Cook, 2008).

## Chapter 36: Shalom Creation Shops

1. James Hunter introduces the language of "faithful presence" in his book *To Change the World* (New York: Oxford University Press, 2010), 237ff. He writes,

"Faithful presence in our spheres of influence does not imply passive conformity to the established structures. Rather, within the dialectic between affirmation and antithesis, faithful presence means a constructive resistance that seeks new patterns of social organization that challenge, undermine, and otherwise diminish oppression, injustice, enmity, and corruption and, in turn, encourage harmony, fruitfulness and abundance, wholeness, beauty, joy, security, and well-being" (247–48).

## Chapter 37: Practicing the Presence of Church

1. Eugene Peterson, *Practice Resurrection* (Grand Rapids: Eerdmans, 2010), 11–12.

## Chapter 39: Practicing Three Things

1. For a biblical analysis of this, see "Walter Brueggemann on the Primary Marks of the Church," www.youtube.com/watch?v=GY73t_yMbLc, uploaded on June 20, 2009.

## Chapter 40: Presence for the Sake of the World

1. "Whenever we think about God, we need to add the words, 'the mission of the Triune God within all of creation.' Whenever we talk about the gospel, we need to add the words, 'for the sake of the world.' Whenever we discuss the church, we need to add the words 'sent into the world to participate fully in God's mission.' Our view of God is not complete without having the world in view, with God in relationship to it as both Creator and Redeemer. The gospel is not fully the gospel if it does not have the whole of creation as its horizon. The church is not fully the church if it does not seek to bring redemption to bear on every dimension of life" (Craig Van Gelder, "For the Sake of the World," in *The Evangelizing Church: A Lutheran Contribution*, ed. Richard Bliese and Craig Van Gelder [Minneapolis: Augsburg Fortress, 2005], 51).

For more than twenty years, **Scott Boren** has been working with churches to help them develop effective community through small groups that are on mission. This focus has required him to develop expertise in the areas of church leadership, church organization, change management, discipleship, and of course, small group dynamics and small group leadership. He has consulted with churches from thirty-five members to ten thousand members to help them develop and implement small groups that are on mission in their neighborhoods.

For six years, he served as one of the pastors at Woodland Hills Church in Saint Paul, MN, in the capacity of the community pastor and most recently as one of the teaching pastors.

He is the author or coauthor of eight different books, including *Missional Small Groups*, *Introducing the Missional Church* (with Alan Roxburgh), *The Relational Way*, and *MissioRelate*.

The best thing about his life is the community he shares with his family, which includes wife Shawna and their four children.

You can contact Scott directly at mscottboren@gmail.com.

Follow him on Twitter at @mscottboren or read his blog at www.mscottboren.com.

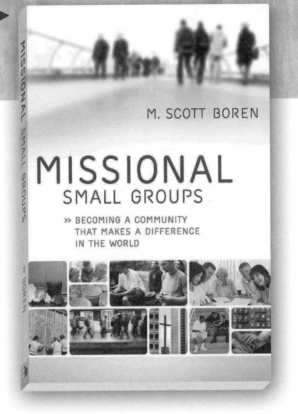

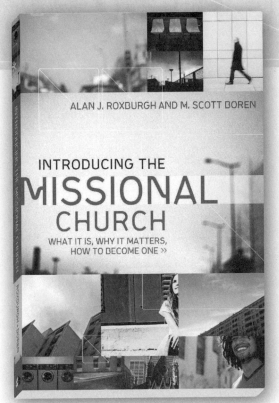